The Wingman's Handbook

A guide to teenage romance by a teenage romantic

MICHELLE Y KWOK

Wingman, (n):

A role that a person may take when a friend needs support with approaching romantic partners.

Acknowledgements

Behind every writer is a team of supporters. Because the subject of this book is particularly close to my heart, I want to express my gratitude to everyone who has made an impact on my life and allowed me to create this book.

A big thank you to my high school friends and everyone whose high-school experiences I've collected for this book. Whether you were romantically-involved with someone else or with me, you have all played a larger role in my life than you could ever imagine. Every moment of joy and pain I saw, every mistake and success I witnessed, served as fuel powering my mind as I put words to paper. Without you, there would be no *Wingman's Handbook*.

Thank you to Mrs Dunlop, my senior English teacher. Mrs Dunlop didn't just teach me English, she transformed my life and inspired me to be whatever I wanted to be. In my five years at Mansfield State High, I learnt a lot about life, both positive and negative, and this was also where most of my experiences took place.

I'm very grateful to my parents and my sister, because they were the first people to be on board when I told them my concept. They helped me do research and draw up plans on how I can work towards the goal of publication. I would have been kidding myself if I thought I could do that all alone. Towards the late production period, I was starting to suffer from imposter syndrome but they helped me to snap out of it. Thank you to all of the beta readers and other contributors. A project is a big machine, but each individual cog helps to make it work.

Finally, I need to thank you as the reader. You are all young lovers with millions of possibilities in life. A book is just a vehicle, but you are the driver that can take it to new levels in your life.

Table of Contents

Introduction 1

Part 1 – Just Before We Really Get Into It 4
    Safety Brief Before We Get Into It 4
    Inhale What is Love? 7
    Your Guide to Pre-Teen Infatuation 9
    Your Guide to the Teenage Shitstorm 12

Part 2 – Setting the Scene 15
    Taste and Preferences 15
        Gender and Identity 16
        Now That's Problematic! 19
    What is this feeling, so sudden and new? 23
        Types of Crushes 23
        The Forget/Pursue Dichotomy 26
    Are You Wasting Your Time? 30

Part 3 – Let's Work on Yourself 33
    General Appearance 33
    Personality 37
        Right here, right now 37
        The Power of Charisma 41
        Strengths & Weaknesses 42

Are You Ready for Love? 44

Part 4 – Now You Think They're The One, Do You? 46
The Road to Pursuit 46

Are You Playing This Game on High Difficulty? (LGBT) 49

The Chess Game of Flirting..52

Strategies 55

    The Do's and Don'ts of Going After Someone....................55

    101 Pickup Lines..55

    101 Icebreakers 64

    The 20-question method...70

    Five Sweet Brain Tricks 72

Friendship, Just the Perfect Blend-Ship 75

Part 5 – It Takes a Spark 79
The Leap 79

The Baby Steps of Baby Steps 86

Limits and Pacing 88

Dating from the Same School?..89

Taking the L 92

Part 6 – A Free Shot of Oxytocin 94
Hormones, Our Little Workers 94

Love Science 95

    The Hormone's Game 95

The Five Love Languages 98
    Rosetta Stone 98
    Makes and Breaks...101
50 Ways to say I Love You 103
The Power of Touch 107
    Touch Zones..108
Love Addiction...113
Withdrawal...116
Relationship Dynamics (LGBT) 117

Part 7 – Living the Honeymoon 119
The Butterflies 119
The Gist..123
    The Internet..123
    The Parental Units..125
The Ingredients to a Healthy Relationship 131
First Things First 135
Relationship Check-Up...139
    Maintenance Checklist 139
Love Blindness..141
50 Relationship Red Flags 145

Part 8 – The Long Haul of Death................................ 149
When the Well Runs Dry 149

Love is Not Lost, Just Evolved 150

Unfortunate Downfalls of the High-School Sweethearts ... 152

Forever means Forever 160

A Summary of What You'll Need 161

Quick Relationship Troubleshooting 163

Meet Me in the Ring! 168

The Hardest Word 176

The Way the Cookie Crumbles 179

Preparing for the Inevitable 179

The Break-Up Checklist 182

Doing the Do 183

The Silent Hand 186

The Ingredients of an Abusive Relationship 186

Push and Pull 187

The Origin of the Abuser 190

Get Over It 195

The Five Stages of Grief 195

Moving On 197

Surprising Benefits of Losing Love 205

Part 9 – Manuals and More 208

Grooming and Appearance 209

Decoding Dress Code 209

How to Tie a Tie 210

How to Roll Up your Sleeves 218

How to Walk in Heels 220

The Colour Wheel 221

Manner and Lifestyle 224

Meal Etiquette 224

Flower Language (basics) 233

How to Sew a Button 235

How to Waltz 236

How to Take Good Photos 240

People and Relationships 251

The Art of Assertiveness 251

How to Console a Partner 261

Saying No 266

How to be a Good Listener 269

The Four Styles of Responding to Good News 271

How to Kiss (Well) 277

Part 10 – Earning Your Wings 282
The Art of Third Wheeling 282

Traits of a Good Wingman 287

What's the Sitch? 288

Intel 290

- Guru 292
- Backup 296
- Support 298
- When to Intervene 301
  - Three Types of Risk Perception 304
  - Body Language Signs 306
- Your Final Dose of Wisdom 312
  - 101 – Make your Own Wingman Kit 320

Closing Words **322**

Introduction

It's 2012.

Image-macro memes were still a thing. Gangnam Style had just come out and invented viral YouTube videos. Life was simple.

And there I was. 11 years old, still in primary school, and had never experienced a single traumatic event yet. At this age, we were starting to experience the wrath of puberty. Barely anybody took it well. It was definitely the war of hormones against the world's population of pre-teens. With my crooked teeth, poor eyesight and bad skin, I was a diamond in the rough, a pearl in the making, deep inside an oyster. In this ugly, nonsense time of our lives, the spring of adolescence was approaching, and the winter of childhood was leaving.

At 11 years old, you didn't have to worry about what university you wanted to go to, or what tax bracket you were in. That's grown-up stuff. But for some strange reason, grown-up stuff had the exact same appeal to us as a flower to a bee. We loved that shit. But what I loved the most about grown-ups wasn't their careers or responsibilities, obviously.

It was their love.

I was so obsessed with romance, I could remember the exact moment the chemicals in my brain aligned to produce the feelings of infatuation on a certain someone who wasn't even physically there. It would happen just because someone mentioned his name. And for your information, I had straight up hated him for the last 2 years because he bullied me. I know it sounds insane, but I can remember the moment as though it was yesterday. That's just how it is. And straight after that incident, my life was changed forever. I could feel just how powerful this attachment was. It was like I was possessed; first in the way my thoughts on him were able to change with a snap of the fingers, and then how this entire thing would haunt my life for the next three years. In hindsight, my attraction to him was completely pointless. I've had a few meaningful, diverse relationships since then, so I know that for sure. But back then, I was having the time of my life. It was just so fun thinking about love and everyone wanted to get a taste of it.

So in the same year I was 11 and caught serious feelings for the first time, I dedicated myself to figuring out just what on earth was happening in my head. Then with this knowledge, I 'helped' others around me. But obviously, what would I know? We were all just kids who had no clue how anything worked. Despite that, I still tried my best to play matchmaker. And I guess I just never stopped. All these years later, I've learned so much but I know I still have a lot more to learn.

I'm not a psychologist; I've only read a few research papers and did a few short courses in psychology here and there. But I have a thirst for knowledge. My sister used to joke that I was a walking encyclopaedia. I'm a regular person, just like you. I feel ecstatic when I fall in love and hurt when I am rejected. But somehow, this only makes me want to talk to you more. Everything in this book is what I've seen, felt and thought throughout my life up until now. That's it. I have no desire to sugar-coat my words or to further twist the already twisted portrayals of love we see in society. I don't want to sell you a magic love potion that will make you irresistible or crush your self-esteem with unrealistic cynicism. I just want to tell you what you'll need to know, and how to make things work.

So, my dear reader, this is *The Wingman's Handbook*.

Welcome aboard.

Part 1

Just Before We Really Get into It

Safety Brief Before Take Off

I feel as though there are some things I need to talk about before you really get comfy with this book. Just a little bit of housekeeping, and some nice contextual information to set the mood for us. I can already see your eyes starting to wander off. Please, I know everyone prefers to ignore disclaimers and terms & conditions, but I highly recommend that you take some time to read the following. Please?

1. This book is separated into ten parts, and these are further split into sections. You're currently on the first part. Each part covers a different topic of love. The parts are in a rough chronological order, so I highly recommend that you read front-to-back on your first reading. Then the second time, you can read it however you like. This book is also organised so that when you have to be a wingman for others, you can flick straight to relevant pages. Also, there are many interactive activities in the book, so if you are reading from an online source or want to keep your hardcopy reusable, copy and print out the activity pages.

2. I would like to reiterate that I am not a psychologist, and do not have official credentials on the subjects of sociology, psychology and biology. That means this book isn't going to

be cited in anyone's thesis any time soon. The aim of this book is not to contribute to the academic research of human psychology, but rather a collection of guides and commentary for young people, especially those that are just starting to dabble in the world of romance. Remember, I'm a young person myself, and I still have lots to learn. This book is comprised of, I'd say, roughly 60% my personal commentary and 40% external sources. These are reputable sources that are from official websites, psychology papers and whatnot, which I believe have aided me in supplying the most relevant and useful knowledge. For any parts of my book that I've consulted a source for, full credit goes to the original content creators. All credit for the stock images go to the photographers on Pexels. The text and images I've collected are protected under Fair Use for research purposes, so please don't sue me.

3. I strive for inclusivity in this handbook. I personally believe that love is a limitless force and isn't something society can control by their own definitions. Therefore, I have kept this book as gender neutral as I can. Anyone can benefit from the information I provide here. I will also refrain from defaulting to traditional gendered stereotypes, which is a downfall for many other guides out there. Who cares if you don't fit the mould? You're here to find out how to find love, and that's all that I'm going to tell you.

4. You'd normally expect sex advice in a guide about love, because those things always go hand in hand (or that's what society thinks). But spoiler alert, there isn't going to be a lot about sex here. That's because I don't feel qualified or confident to help. Sex is a subject that is a lot more sensitive than romance, mostly because it ties into more than one dimension of health (physical, spiritual, mental, emotional), so that would take a whole separate book if I really were to write about it.

5. This book contains anecdotes of events and people. That's because I'm a real person and I've seen things. However, I probably don't know you, so if you feel like any of the names and events resembles real-life people and events you know about, then chances are it's all purely coincidental, alright? This book also delves into mature themes, such as abuse, sexual assault and mental illness. Also, there's a little bit of coarse language, but just a little. Reader's discretion is advised.

Inhale What is Love?

I think that another thing we can discuss before the book starts is love itself. If you're more academically inclined, you'd define love as a very strong and positive mental and emotional state. It's a cocktail of 'good-feeling' hormones. This attraction, the romantic kind, is used to form bonds with a mate. It's good to know what love is, because it's so damn powerful. It's really cheesy and has been done to death by the film industry (see Interstellar), suggesting that love can fix everything. But you know what? Love probably can. That is, if it is actual love. Saying nice words to someone or sleeping with them isn't going to fix them. Real love is one of the most complicated concepts known to man.

I was once invited to a conference for 'smart' year 10 kids where we discussed philosophy, time and government. It was certainly an enlightening experience, but in hindsight, seemed a little pretentious. At one point we discussed the topic of love, and I was invited to add my input. As a 15-year-old who knew nothing, I took the mic, faced the audience of 300 other individuals and said the first thought that popped into my head - a quote I had read somewhere on the Internet: 'In a Universe where nothing is certain, love is. The certainty that love possesses is its nature of uncertainty.'

To be honest, I had no idea what was saying back then. I just thought it sounded profound. What the quote means is that the world is crazy and literally anything can happen at any time. You're not certain that today it will rain, or if you'll wake up tomorrow morning. You won't be able to say for sure that you'll live to 85, or that you'll get a dog when you're 18. You can argue with me on this all day – yes, there's medicine, a weather forecast, common sense, that type of stuff – but when were those things ever 100% accurate? There's only one thing in the world that is certain, yep, 100%. And do you know what it is? It's uncertainty. You know for sure that you're not gonna be in full control of your life, no matter how many bath bombs you add to your exquisite 'I've-got-my-shit-together' skincare routine. With this, you can say for sure that anything goes. And that doesn't have to be doom and gloom. As uncertainty is the only certainty in the world, it means that our potential is boundless, there's nothing to define us except ourselves.

So now back to love. Why's it uncertain? Because no matter how many PhD's you have, how many research papers you've done and how many brains you've dissected, love will forever be a mystery. Just take a trip around Google and you'll see how love compels people to do extraordinary things that they probably wouldn't have done without it motivating them. Then you will also see the weird ways love settles or disappears. There are couples that meet in primary school and stay together forever. Then there are people that don't find each other until they're on their deathbeds. Sometimes, people never find love at all. Love is weird and a power that would be better left as it is. It would be a waste of time to fully understand it. This is why the best we can do is to condition ourselves to love, and not the other way around.

Your Guide to the Pre-Teen Infatuation

Teenagers are notorious to the older demographics. They're seen as a horny, stupid group that think they're above adult law, yet they don't have the intellect to actually be an adult. But have you seen pre-teens? Especially in this day and age? They are way worse. This society is experiencing a phenomenon I call '<u>accelerated maturation</u>', where the normalising of what would be considered 'taboo' and 'adult' subjects have caused children to be exposed to them faster. This is why you see a lot of those memes lying around where 90's kids post a picture of their embarrassing 12-year-old self with metal-clad teeth, compared side-by-side with a very carefully constructed photo of a current Instagram model of roughly the same age. The meme's caption is usually something like, 'Wow, look at kids nowadays! Back in my day we looked more like actual kids!' It's crazy, and even a little terrifying, that this is happening, but it is absolutely not the kid's fault. In fact, it's society's fault that children are experiencing an accelerated maturation. They've grown up in a world full of colourful sex, drugs and violence. The desire to become adults faster has been ingrained into their tiny brains. You can start even by the fact that preschools ask kids what they want to be when they grow up.

Pre-teens are a vulnerable bunch. The way accelerated maturation hits them is not through pretending to be grown-ups, but rather the persuasion that they are already teenagers physically and mentally. This sets them up on a VERY dangerous platform for paedophiles and exploitation, but that's a topic for another day. A big part of being a teen/young-adult is romance. Naturally, the pre-teens and tweens would want a scoop of that too. Now don't get me wrong, pre-teens are experiencing the very tip of puberty at that moment, so sexual curiosity is very normal. Their banter about crushes and daydreaming about soulmates is pretty standard. However, the looming claw of society is what makes this all not ok. It sets up high expectations that exceed normal. It grooms them to want things that they don't and shouldn't need. And last of all, it promises them the pretty picture of love by showing them lovers that are from a completely different age group (therefore different maturity level, physical level etc.). The truth is romantic love does not exist at this stage in life. Let me say it again. Romantic love. Does not. Exist. At this stage in life. You can tell me, 'I met this guy when we were both 11 and now we're graduating high school and we're still together. What are you talking about?' Yeah, but what you experienced at 11 years old was not love, but rather a bundle of strong feelings that your biology has conditioned you to feel. We have a word for it, and it is called <u>infatuation.</u> (To read more on whether you have an infatuation or you've fallen in love, go to part 2).

Infatuations are not an evil thing. Love is very difficult to achieve, and love can even develop from an infatuation. For pre-teens, infatuations don't lead to romance. Many of them are dead ends, regardless of the fact that the person lost interest and was disappointed. There's no official measure, but infatuations can last from just a quick one for a few days to years. I had many emotional sparks throughout my primary school life, but my very first infatuation struck me violently out of nowhere. I can recall the exact moment my hormones clicked, and it was absolutely wild. Eventually, the infatuation came to an end a few years later, but only because I was distracted by the stress of adjusting to high school.

If you know a pre-teen who you are concerned about, this part is for you. Giving them a reality check may be helpful to ensure they are aware of their risks. While they are told maturity is their ability to down alcohol and engage in serious relationships, real maturity is their ability to act safely after assessing their mental intelligence and evaluating the external stimuli they are given. Completely shunning their feelings is not a good move. Remember, pre-teen/tween 'love' is not terrible in nature, but being vigilant is essential to reduce emotional and mental pain. Steering clear of society's mask is important for these vulnerable, increasingly mature beings.

Your Guide to the Teenage Shitstorm

Eventually, all pre-teens grow up and become teenagers. 13-year-olds constantly like to argue that they're teenagers because their age has 'teen' in it. Sorry, but a suffix isn't going to change the fact you're not any different to people one or two years younger than you. For the sake of convenience, I'm going to classify teenagers as 16-18-year-olds. This is also helpful because 16 is the age of consent here (and in most countries), so it won't feel weird if I mention sex later on.

Adolescence is one of the most chaotic stages in life. We are constantly trapped under immense pressure by both our own peers and grown-ups. Identity – all aspects of it – becomes extremely valuable, even too valuable here. It is a pandemic, therefore it is too late for anyone to fix that. Tweens don't immediately mature and become hardened love experts once they become teens (that was something I had to take myself out of). Infatuations still exist here, but with a little chance, just a tiny miraculous one, love may manifest. Remember, even in adulthood, love doesn't come easily, so the fact that late adolescence may be a chance for it to appear is very significant.

The main difference between teen infatuation and tween infatuation is that for teens, it leans more towards sexual lust than anything. People are described not so much as 'cute' but rather 'hot'. You don't want them to hold your hand; you want them to bed you (unless you're asexual, but you get the gist). I made a gross generalisation there, but the idea of wanting to sleep with someone may not be so strongly desired in tweens (though sexualisation through accelerated maturation may change that very soon). This increases the amount of risks for teenagers. When you're adding your body on top of your emotional and mental wellbeing, the stakes are gonna be high. In case you're not sure what I mean, here are some risks:

- STD's
- Intoxicated sex, which leads to all the other risks here
- Sexual assault
- Injury through inexperience
- Reputation damage, both through rumours and truths
- Unwanted pregnancy
- Emotional distress
- Spontaneous combustion (you never know)

Important note: Sex is not wrong! Teenagers have sex, that's true, but with careful measures and trust, these risks can be averted. Now back to the programme.

The toxicity of the dating and sex culture is insane. Teenagers are often put into 'damned if you do, damned if you don't' situations. For example, if you've never slept with anyone, you're a virgin loser. If you have slept with more than one person, you're probably easy. Everyone around you has probably dated, because it's a 'normal' thing and you're the only one that hasn't ... or you have a romantic partner and everyone around you teases you for 'betraying your mates'. Even if you were to win the favour of others' admiration of your prudence or prowess, you're still basking in a gross glorification of love.

The best way for you to get through teenage romance is to be free. Explore your sexuality and preferences. Your heart may break a lot, but that is all in the process of life, I guess. And yes, there are people in high school that seem to be utterly in love already. They've probably dated longer than the average lifespan of a teen romance (i.e. 2 months to 2 years), so everyone thinks they're going to live happily ever after. When they reach the final year of high school, there's a special term for the couple, and a very likely tragedy (you can read more on this in part 8).

Part 2

Setting the Scene

In this chapter, we'll be looking at the most important person in your life – you! Getting to know more about your feelings is going to help a lot with understanding other people's. As they say, it's important to love yourself as much as you love others.

Taste and Preferences

Imagine if you could have a catalogue in your hand. And inside you could sort people by hair colour, eye colour, how many spoons of sugar they want in their tea etc. Everyone is so damn unique, you could probably spend 60 years looking at all the possible combinations. Taste and preferences are natural for human romantic love. To look at this from the biological point of view, this is a form of genetic selection. Animals choose a suitable mate based on their physical and genetic traits. This is so that the offspring will hopefully inherit these desirable genes. Sounds all nice and simple, but humans being humans have made their very own complex-as-hell system.

So now enough of the biology lesson, you're probably here to learn and assess what your OWN tastes and preferences are, right?

Gender and Identity

I am not intending to turn this into yet another biology/sociology lesson, so here's a super useful chart.

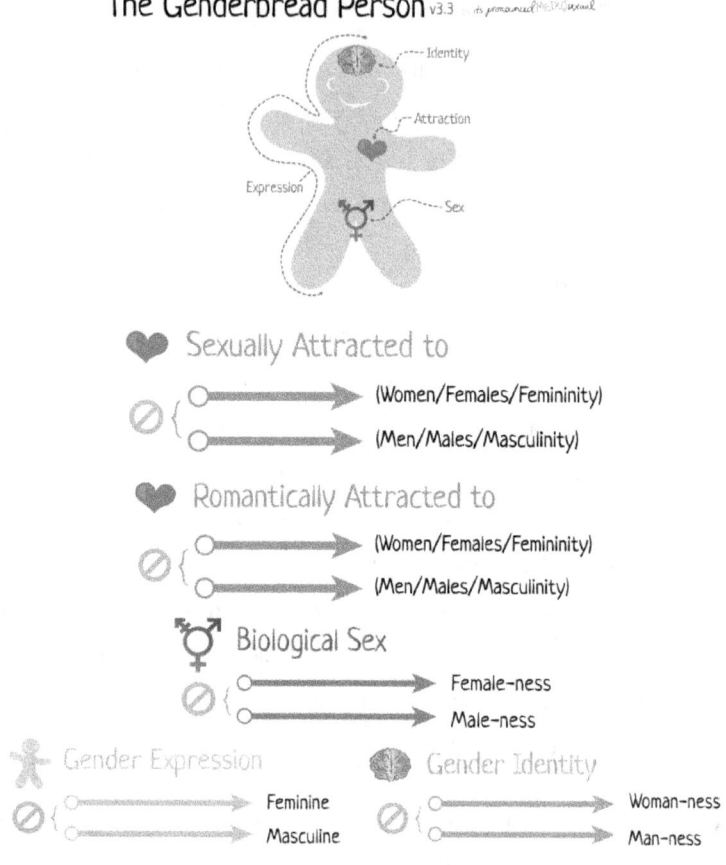

As you can see, identities can be pretty diverse. Figure out what gender/traits you're attracted to. If the chart is too confusing here are some of the 'mainstream' sexual identities that you may identify as:

- ❖ **Heterosexual (straight):** You're only attracted to the opposite sex.

- ❖ **Bisexual:** Traditionally, referred to attraction of both male and female.

- ❖ **Pansexual:** Traditionally, having no regards to gender for attraction.

- ❖ **Homosexual (gay/lesbian):** You're only attracted to the same sex.

- ❖ **Asexual:** You experience little to no sexual attraction.

There has been A LOT of discourse over the real definitions of these as gender theory is constantly revised over the years. Because some believe bisexuality enforces the gender binary (which a big no-no for many modern queers), they define it as liking your own gender and another gender. But the problem with that is it would almost be the same thing as pansexuality. This would mean that one of the labels have to go, and that would be called 'erasure'. As you can see, the whole thing is super confusing and maybe better left alone.

Labels can be both harmful and beneficial for a person using them. In more recent times, many prefer to drop labels and go by the umbrella term 'queer' because they feel restricted. This can be especially confining for them if their identity changes (sexual and gender identities can be fluid). On the other hand, these labels built the foundation of the LGBT community. Some people like labels because it makes them feel included and not alone when they meet others of the same label. Whether you choose to adopt one or not, that's up to you.

If you're not sure what gender/identity you're really attracted to, just take your time. Forcing yourself to be something (especially straight) is bad. Don't do it, because when you start feeling things that are different from what you expect, it's going be a bad experience. You might feel guilt, confusion and anger. A quote I love from Amy Ordman is, 'Labels are like shoes sizes. They can change throughout your life but each previous one got you to where you are now.'

Now That's Problematic!

We are all entitled to the freedom of choice, so no one can tell us who we find attractive or unattractive. However, the media does pull our puppet strings in this aspect. Get to know the difference between what you should find attractive and what you REALLY find attractive. But, like all things in the world, there's a limit. Believe it or not, there is a fine line between preference and straight-up discrimination (again, this is an unfortunate doing of society). It's difficult to exactly answer 'what requirements are problematic though?' because a lot of the time it is not the actual category itself, but the attitude.

Here's a basic list of preferences that people might have:

- Gender
- Age
- Hobbies
- Background
- Race
- Height
- Body shape
- Sexual history

And here's a list of preferences that can get problematic:

- Gender
- Age
- Hobbies
- Background
- Race
- Height
- Body shape
- Sexual history

Notice anything? They're the same. Any preference can become discriminatory. Another thing is that it can also turn into 'fetishisation', which is a fancy word for 'I am just attracted to a feature of a person and not the actual person'.

Let's look at some examples using the table below:

Preference	Problematic
"I want to date women."	"I would never date a trans woman cause they're not real women."
"I want a guy that is tall."	"Men shorter than six feet aren't real men."
"I would prefer to date within my own race."	"I'd avoid dating black people because they're unattractive."
"I'm attracted to girls that are more toned."	"Fat girls are disgusting, I'd never date them."
"Personally, I'd like to date someone that is a virgin."	"I would never be with a non-virgin, they're all sluts."

The 'problematic' section shows us what happens when someone shows more than just a preference. Instead of just stopping at 'I'm not attracted to them', they take the extra mile to generalise everyone that has that trait. Now that's a big yikes, isn't it? The right thing to do would be to have the preferences and move on. Many of the preferences that people are prejudiced against – like race and physical appearance – aren't even things the other person can control.

You'll notice in the following table that the preference column remains the same, but I've put in new problematic phrases.

Preference	Problematic
"I want to date women."	"If my girlfriend was bi that would be so hot."
"I want a guy that is tall."	"I only talk to tall guys because I know they're hung down there."
"I would prefer to date within my own race."	"I find Japanese girls very exotic."
"I'm attracted to girls that are more toned."	"I love myself some girls with all the right body proportions."
"Personally, I'd like to date someone that is a virgin."	"It would be very exhilarating for me to be a virgin's first."

Instead of putting down what the person finds unattractive, they're raising the preference onto an unnaturally creepy pedestal. Fetishisation is mostly sexual - 'I find this trait very sexy' - or maybe not - 'I want to date an Asian guy because they're smart'.

It is okay to have preferences because, after all, physical attraction isn't something we can control. However, discrimination and fetishisation isn't going to make those that fit your criteria flattered. In fact, it'll just make them feel uncomfortable and demeaned. That's because the message you're sending them is that you only like the few traits you've reduced them to, and not their entire personality. Love isn't going to work if you choose a single apple you want then cut down the whole tree.

So, let's take a moment for you to think about all the traits you're into, and ask yourself if you're being prejudiced or not.

What is this feeling, so sudden and new?

Ah yes, one of the most fun and painful bits of the whole love thing: crushes. As messed up as this sounds, crushes were probably one of the major reasons I bothered to wake up in the morning and go to school. On a social level, this can be attributed to the fact that it's a complex and fun thing to work out. The media keeps selling it to us as something super fun. On a technical level, mundane school life can barely reward the same level of satisfaction and happiness as a romantic crush. During periods of time where I had no crushes, school was actually really boring. Sure, friend groups and everything still brought in some social satisfaction, but nothing could compare to the bittersweet game of romantic pursuit. Now, I know that there's stuff to do that is more important than crushes when you're in high school (like schoolwork), but still, we've all had our scoop of allowing our minds to zone out and swoon over someone.

Types of Crushes

Crushes don't just apply to peers. There are actually a lot of different types. The word itself can be used as an umbrella term for any type of infatuation with someone (sexual desire is a whole new concept called lust). In nature, the onset of sexual maturation means that it's time to search for a potential mate. That's why we see crushes happening around the same time we hit puberty – the 6-year-olds holding hands and saying 'this is my boyfriend' don't count. They don't even know what commitment *is*. When you start to look for a potential mate, you'll start to notice appealing traits in others that you probably wouldn't have thought about when you were younger. That's why your crush can be on anyone, regardless of whether you've known them for a long time or you've just seen them around town.

Identity

Psychology separates crushes as two main types: identity and romantic. Both of them require some sort of infatuation and idealisation, but identity crushes (which in several cultures aren't even called 'crushes' because the term is used exclusively for romance) are on a desire to become the person. There isn't necessarily a romantic or sexual drive behind it, though there can be. You can actually split down identity crushes into different scenarios:

> **Regular Identity Crush** - Wanting to be like a particular person they find appealing.
>
> **Celebrity Crush** - Admiring an attractive and appealing celebrity.
>
> **Stranger Crush** - Seeing an attractive and cool stranger in public.
>
> **Authority (?) Crush** - You know the ones where you like a teacher or someone above you? Yeah, those ones.

Identity crushes are pretty major during youth. Why? Because it's a period of time where we're trying to figure out our *own* identities. We start to wonder who we are, and care about how other people view us. As the influence of parents start to fade, our role models are replaced with peers and people in the media.

Romance

Now on to the romantic crush (probably the main reason you're here). A romantic crush is more about wanting to be *with* a person. This is the type of crush you'd describe as causing 'butterflies in your stomach'. This type of feeling can be pretty intense.

As I've mentioned previously, crushes are a mix of infatuation and idealisation. As much as it may feel so in that instance, a crush is NOT love. Idealisation means that you like what you THINK they're like, and not what they actually ARE like. A large part of this infatuation comes from enigma. We wonder what their hobbies are, what's on their mind when they stare dramatically out of the window, what it would be like to hold their hand. So, we are motivated to find out. Now the problem here is that we think we have found the answers ('he likes animals!'), when in reality we've just projected values on them that we WISHED they had ('He hasn't kicked a dog yet so hopefully he likes animals'). The reason why crushes have a short lifespan is because the enigma fades. Psychologists have decided that a crush typically lasts a maximum of 4 months. Any longer than that, and you're in love. But that still doesn't mean your judgement isn't clouded. We eventually get to know the crush and the magic wears off. It pulls us back into reality and we realise they weren't many of the things we thought they were. Some accredit it to the fact they've changed, but for you more self-aware folks (anyone reading this book is self-aware), you'll know that it's your brain masking your perception (when you're in love, Love Blindness plays a big role. More on that in part 7).

Now, that's not necessarily a bad thing because that fading of magic happens in committed relationships too (read more about in When the Well Runs Dry, part 8).

The Forget/Pursue Dichotomy

When you've got a crush, what are you supposed to do? I've personally developed something called the Forget/Pursue model to sort out crushes. The only two true possible actions a person may take while being infatuated with someone is either to forget (avoid advances) or pursue (accelerate advances). These two broad terms cover most actions, but there are exceptions. Passive actions such as visualising your wedding, writing self-insert fanfiction with them in it (please do not EVER do that) or talking to your friends about them are neutral – no matter how 'forward' they are. That's because the forget/pursue model is about what you ultimately want to do with the individual, not with the idea of a crush. If you're not sure what you feel, ask yourself this question:

Can I picture myself in a relationship with them? Will I make it happen?

If you answered yes, that means you're on the pursue route. If you answered no or not sure, then you're most likely going to end up in the forget route. Sometimes people make sudden epiphanies and switch. A good way to get rid of superficial infatuations is the 24-hour test. Force yourself to abstain from thoughts of them for a day (if your mind starts to drift in that direction, cut the thought off). If by the end of the period you're still interested in them, and don't particularly want to forget them, move on to the pursuit route.

Forget Route

To forget, or more accurately 'wait out' a crush can be very painful. I'm just going to put that out there first. It's especially painful if you've had a crush for longer than 4 months because feelings in that situation become much more intensified. There are various reasons you may choose the forget route:

- ❖ You're crushing on someone that you shouldn't (e.g. a friend's ex).
- ❖ You're not interested in a relationship at the moment.
- ❖ You consciously know they're not a good person.
- ❖ You know the chance of getting with them is close to zero.
- ❖ You know they're already taken or have rejected you before.

The forget route is actually harder than the pursue route because it requires self-actualisation. You need to be able to free yourself away from the love-blindness and credit your hormones for your unfortunate choice in attraction. Instagram frequently calls liking something 'catching feelings', and I can't agree with this term more.

Waiting out a crush is hard, but unless they suddenly do something so horrendous that it instantly makes you change your mind, there's no other way. So here is how you can make the most of the forget route:

1. **Admit to yourself you have a crush first** - Failing to do this makes you unable to set up the forget/pursue dichotomy

because there's no starting ground.

2. **Take few steps back** – Increase the distance between you and them. If you've already invested a lot of your time into them, withdraw it slowly. Removing the physical issue won't immediately make you move on, but it does clear your head to follow the next steps.

3. **Brainstorm their less attractive traits** – Everyone has pros and cons, but for crushes your brain always blocks out the cons. Thinking about their cons removes the infatuation filter and paints them once again in the light of a normal human being.

4. **Distract yourself** – Not with other people but get into something that will compete for brain space. Perhaps get into a fandom or reinforce your already-existing fandoms.

5. **Get a new target** – This can backfire easily so use with discretion. Finding a new, more appropriate love interest will quickly stamp out this current crush.

Pursue Route

Now this is where the fun begins. To pursue means to actually put effort into turning the crush into something more. While forgetting is more mentally draining, pursuing is more physically draining for obvious reasons.

To follow this route, here's a summary of what to do:

1. **Be sure** – You need to make sure you've given yourself a green light to do this. Of course, you can pull out anytime –

there's no contract or anything – but nobody likes to waste their time and brain space.

2. **Interact with them** – Let them know you exist if they don't already. You don't need to immediately dive into their personal life. In fact, even a simple 'good morning' will work. Start small.

3. **Find out if it's mutual** – If they flirt back, instigate conversations and other interactions, then it looks like you've already won half the battle. Be careful not to mix up signs of innocent friendliness and interest, or you'll be embarrassed later on.

4. **Stop immediately if they show resistance** – It is important you must understand how to stop as soon as they display discomfort or rejection. If you keep trying, then you've become a harasser.

5. **Make the leap** – On the other hand, if things seem right, consider making the move to ask them out.

The entirety of part 4 is dedicated to the pursuit route, so check it out for more information.

Are You Wasting your Time?

From all of this, it must feel pretty overwhelming and discouraging to know that at this stage, any romantic attraction can be a gamble between one of life's best reward (love) and absolutely nothing (infatuation). And no one wants to waste their time either, right? So, what's an easy way to know if you're feeling love or infatuation? Although all the previous sections make it sound like everything is super complex, you can differentiate between the two with the easy-to-remember acronym: **EDICTS**.

Expectations

Infatuations often leave us thinking about a person in a distorted way. That means we may see them as much better than they are. And then when you start dating, expectations happen in the form of their interactions with us. This leaves us vulnerable to the disappointments and disputes. When we're in love, we're more prepared for the reality that relationships encounter lots of obstacles and are willing to work around it. This requires the need to discard an expectation that the relationship will be 'perfect'. With an infatuation, it is too easy to let the mind run free and imagine only happy-ever-afters.

Duration

This one is pretty obvious but love lasts much longer than infatuation. That's because the feelings behind an infatuation will eventually wear off with time while love is more persistent. We talked about this in part 1.

Interest

Sure, you like them, but *what* do you like about them? You can't say that you fell in love with someone because of 'the way they talk' or 'their eyes' or something vague like that. You can, of course, *appreciate* these things but when you're in love, you'll find yourself giving different answers.

Connection

Adding on to the previous section, the interest you have in a person you love is definitely going to be about who they are in general. Yes, infatuation requires a connection too, but the thread that binds you to them is thin. When you're in love, the connection will be a feeling that just kind of drifts along. If you both have a sense of unspoken understanding, then you're in love.

Time

How long did it take for you to fall for them? If they were pretty much a stranger when it began, then I can assure you that it's an infatuation. That's because at first the only traits you'd see from them, as a stranger, is their outer self, which links back to the 'Interest' section. Alternatively, if you find your attraction to them is uncontrollably fast, meaning you went from 'this person seems neat' to 'I want to marry them right now and have their babies', in just a matter of days then maybe it isn't love.

Security (applies only if you are dating)

Every relationship must endure the tides of time and not all of them survive. If you looked at your current attractions to someone, think: what would happen if something went wrong between us tomorrow? How strong are the foundations of your relationship? Is it fickle enough that pressure will break the two of you up? And most importantly, do you have enough willpower to hold on to the relationship?

It's been quite a few chapters of theory, so in the next chapter we'll be redirecting the focus.

Part 3

Let's Work on Yourself

This chapter's going to be about the most important person ever – you! You see, relationships are a two-way thing, and it starts with what you do with yourself. It's not gonna be easy to find love if you don't love yourself first!

General Appearance

Sorry, but looks do matter after all. It's easy for us to dismiss society as shallow and judging. Since the dawn of history, our expectations of 'beauty' have changed rapidly. With every turn of the century, we've had to conform to those rules that were written by 'no one' and make changes to become a 'someone'. I for one am happy that we've broadened our standards of what's beautiful in this day and age. Our higher acceptance contributes to a more positive society.

But after all, we are animals. And nature dictates that we will choose the most attractive mate. You don't see a peahen saying, "Okay you want to mate, but are you a financially-smart lad? Are you emotionally sensitive?" Sure, we are highly-developed beings and have the ability to judge personality and other inner traits, but you can't tell someone volunteers at an animal shelter just by looking at them for the first time, you know.

So the middle line I'm drawing in this appearance vs personality debate is: both matter, but in different ways. It's a biological response for us to look at things we like looking at. Being an attractive person means you'll be pleasant to look at, pleasant to be *considered*. Come on, I'm sure you'd also buy those cute little Japanese snacks just cause their packaging is super cute and colourful. But after you've become attracted to the person, it's the inner personality that keeps your interest. An attractive person that's a piece of shit is inevitably, well, a piece of shit. Looks won't improve an unattractive personality at all. This is especially important because when we make the transition from infatuation to love, the person's understanding of you will also shift from your exterior self to interior self.

It doesn't hurt to take care of your appearance. Even just grooming and keeping yourself neat and tidy helps, not only for you to attract people, but also to help with your own self-confidence (which is a VERY valuable trait to have because it's also attractive).

You don't have to be James Charles or any other beauty blogger. But everyone should know these simple grooming tips, regardless of your gender.

Skin - During puberty, we go through a lot of hormonal changes and unfortunately that shows on our face. First of all, don't feel bad if you have acne or any other skin problem. At this point, it's not something you can control, and sometimes you may be genetically predisposed. Depending on the nature of your skin, use corresponding products to try to maintain good skin. This means for dry skin, regularly moisturise and use gentle facewash. If you have oily skin/acne, opt for stronger facewash and use water-based moisturiser so it doesn't clog up your pores. Either way, your skin still needs to have moisture constantly because that's what keeps it elastic and glowing healthily. Oh, and exfoliate to remove dead skin and other junk as that will clog up pores and form pimples.

Hair – Wash your hair regularly, but don't overdo it because shampoo dries out your hair. Shampoo goes in your hair roots to soak up the grease and stuff that accumulates at your hair follicles. Conditioner, on the other hand, should be kept away from the scalp. Remember to rinse it all completely off. Ever had an itchy scalp after washing your hair? That's because you didn't wash it off properly. Get to know your hair type and use products accordingly. Same applies with haircuts. Definitely pick a cut that'll give you confidence, but it also has to fit your head shape. Brush or comb your hair regularly.

Smell - Did you know that a person's scent actually has more subconscious power than their appearance? Smell is linked to the part of the brain that processes emotion and memory. You want to make sure that your first impression in their memory has a pleasant place as well as smell. Studies show that unpleasant and bad smells actually send pain signals to the brain to warn us of possible danger. Keep this in mind next time you're smelly and talking to your date – you're actually dealing them *physical pain.* Ouch. You can avoid that by taking regular baths or showers and adding a touch of perfume or cologne of your liking. When it's hot during summer, carry around a cloth or towel to wipe your sweat away. Trust me, stale sweat doesn't smell good and doesn't really look good on your shirt either.

Clothing - We've all heard the saying: 'Style is a way to say who you are without having to speak.' Yes, it is the inside that counts, but you still have to make yourself presentable in the first place. Be on the look-out for new trends and always be open to try new things. But at the same time, don't forget to be you. Because when you wear something that makes you feel confident, your confidence will add to your attractiveness. After all, clothing is another form of self-expression. Even if we don't do it on purpose, the choices we make about what we wear will reflect our personal brand. Oh and fun fact, you can both be yourself and also follow trends! Let's say for example you've always got yourself a peppy aesthetic. Both low-waisted jeans and off-the-shoulder tops are associated with that style, but only one of those is actually trendy right now. You can rock an off-the-shoulder top, which is popular with everyone, but still keep your aesthetic. But remember that your aesthetic may change with time.

Fitness – It's true that society does pressure us into unrealistic body standards. Everyone's body is different, and how fat and muscle is distributed also varies. With that being said, it's important that we still exercise regularly and have a good diet. You don't need to have bulging muscles or a flat stomach, but it's definitely ideal to be able to run up a flight of stairs without your life flashing before your eyes. Poor health does much more damage than you think. It's not just your insides that will suffer, but all the other previous aspects of grooming will be negatively affected too. Being constantly sick and in an unhealthy body can damage your mental state and confidence.

Now that we've got general appearance sorted, let's move onto your inner self.

Personality

Your appearance acts as your packaging. After someone opens the packaging, they will hope the contents are as good as the box advertises. You can almost imagine it like an iceberg. So here's some information about making sure you're an attractive person on the inside.

Right here, right now

"Do not dwell in the past; do not dream of the future, concentrate the mind on the present moment." The Buddha

Ever heard the term 'mindfulness'? Maybe you've heard it once during an assembly and immediately fell asleep because you don't care about the vague Zen stuff that your school tries to teach you. But mindfulness means your ability to focus on the present. We, as humans, have a complex brain that comprehends the past and future.

Next time you reflect on something either before bed or during a boring class, you'll realise that you're almost always either recalling a memory or speculating the future. Why is it good for us to focus on the present? Well, for starters, many of us generate negative emotions from thinking in a different time frame, such as dwelling on a sad memory or worrying about the future. The problem with this is that it's an unproductive activity. What's the point of mulling over a sad point in our life when it's never going to change? And there's a saying that says 'stressing over an impending thing means you have to live through it twice'. Sometimes it's just better to be in the present.

How exactly can we connect the concept of mindfulness to romance? First of all, being mindful eliminates two major barriers to a good love life: past heartbreaks and excessive pressure. Mindfulness redirects your attention to things that really matter; things that are happening now. Research shows that mindfulness improves overall relationship satisfaction and romantic well-being. That's because it makes us better at communication, increases empathy and improves our ability to deal with relationship stress. When you're mindful, you're more ready to pursue and maintain a romantic relationship.

To improve your mindfulness, there are many exercises you can do. The Buddhists cracked the code thousands of years ago by dedicating time in their day to put full awareness on their breathing. They called it meditation. Contrary to popular belief, meditation doesn't just have to be sitting cross-legged for hours. That's a *form* of meditation, but there's many different others that don't include pins and needles in your legs. The method you use doesn't matter because they all take you to the same destination. Another form of meditation I'd like to introduce to you is the mandala. It's the Sanskrit word for circle, a shape that has importance in many major religions and ideologies. They're beautiful, circular patterns. Dedicating some time in your day away from distractions and just putting your energy into colouring one in is an effective way of practicing mindfulness. I've attached one here for you to try, but there's hundreds of different designs you can find on the Internet. Once you're done, you might also want to write down the feelings you have generated in the process.

The end goal isn't for you to finish colouring all the parts as fast as you can. It's an activity for you to focus on the present activity of colouring, and on colouring only. So print out the mandala, break out your colouring pencils and have some relaxing fun.

The Power of Charisma

Just gonna straight up say it but, <u>charisma</u> is probably the most appealing trait in any person. In fact, it is so strong that it can almost override any other characteristics. To put it simply, charisma (also known as charm) is basically attraction in its purest form. Charm is severely underrated because it is widely misunderstood. Unlike beauty or intelligence, it's not easily disputable and most people agree on the same definition of charm. Additionally, it is also easy to learn and develop. To look at it closely, charisma is picked up through little mannerisms, a confident demeanour, friendliness and humour. The trait does not substitute poor looks, but will make the other person focus on the attractiveness of the charming person, as well as ignore flaws. Because of that, charm is very powerful and potentially a dangerous trait to have. Use it wisely.

You may be thinking to yourself, 'but how the heck do I become charismatic? Where do I start?' This trait, like others, can be cultivated early by the environment of upbringing, and also by peer groups a little later on. There are people that are charming without even realising. Charming people naturally liven up a room upon entering and draw people to them. This effect happens regardless of whether the person is deliberately using tricks, or they're just being themselves. Because of that, it's absolutely possible for you to become charming too.

There are numerous traits that are universally considered desirable, such as kindness, confidence and humour. Developing these traits will greatly improve your charm. You can start with small things, like maintaining a gentle smile while talking to people, greeting people regularly (more than just acknowledging their presence) and telling rightfully-placed jokes to decrease tension.

Strengths & Weaknesses

Nobody in this world is perfect. We're all bound to have a mix of good and bad in us. With that being said though, it doesn't mean that you should use that as an excuse to not work on your flaws. Working on a flaw doesn't make you perfect, but it makes you a BETTER person. The keyword is BETTER, because that's an infinite goal with no cap, unlike perfection. You can't say 'I'm more perfect', because perfect is a limit, an end goal. However, you can absolutely say 'I'm better' than I was'.

It's good to know our own strengths and weaknesses so that we won't be taken by surprise. When you're trying to get involved with someone romantically, being aware of your traits will allow both of you to work out problems easier. For example, maybe you know you're easily forgetful. When getting together with someone, you can let them know that. They might be lenient with you for being late to dates, but they will also work with you to fix that flaw. See what I'm getting at?

It's underrated how powerful it can be if you are with someone who is compatible with you in terms of strengths and weaknesses. It means that you have each other's back and your strengths can lift each other up.

Let's do a quick exercise. Make a table and list three strengths and weaknesses. Then beside them, write how the strengths may benefit a relationship, and write how a weakness may possibly be overcome by the strengths in your partner.

If you have trouble filling that table in, that's okay. In the future, you may even find yourself ticking things off and updating the table.

Are You Ready for Love?

Now here's a fun question. After this, we'll finally be moving onto things that are less theory and more about the person you want to date. How exciting is that?

Here's a quick checklist you can complete to save you some time. Only consider starting a relationship when all of those things are ticked off. Otherwise, there can be some rather unpleasant (unpleasant is an understatement) consequences.

- ☐ Will you be able to handle heartbreak without dying figuratively? (We'll talk more about that in part 8.)
- ☐ Can you commit time and effort into another person for a long term?
- ☐ Do you know exactly what you're looking for, and the red flags you want to avoid?
- ☐ Have you assessed your attractions with EDICTS?
- ☐ Are you able to compromise your interests for another person (to a degree)?
- ☐ Do you genuinely want to be in a relationship, free of peer or societal influence?
- ☐ Do you see yourself as presentable, or 'dateable'? (If not, read this whole chapter again.)
- ☐ Is your mind completely free from past relationships? (If applicable?)

If you can't tick everything off immediately, take your time. Come back to this checklist every time you feel you are good enough to check something off. Eventually, you'll find that you've got everything you need to be mentally and physically prepared for a relationship. And when you are, dive into the next chapter.

Part 4

Now You Think They're the One, Do You?

Maybe it was the brief moment your hand touched theirs when you swapped books. Or it's the fleeting, yet irresistible glance you exchanged on your busy commute to class. Oh great. You've caught feelings. Now what? You've read all the previous chapters which focus on *preparing* yourself, but now we will finally take the second step.

The Road to Pursuit

There's a specific reason why I didn't expand on the pursuit route when I explained the dichotomy of forget/pursuit earlier. It's because there's just so much to talk about. The forget route is about cessation, the termination of something. But the pursuit route, oh boy, it opens up a lot more doors. Here's a quick recap of the pursuit route if you're too lazy to flip back:

1. Be sure you want to pursue someone.

2. Interact with the person.

3. Test the waters to see if they like you back.

4. Stop pursuing if they are resistant.

5. When things seem clear, make the leap.

Say you're absolutely ready, you've worked on yourself and you're very sure you want to pursue somebody. The first thing you need to do is assess the person you like. Look at point number 3 and 4. Pursuit is only successful if the person is worth it.

Here's an assessment guide you can use on the person you are interested in.

- ☐ Emotional Availability

    Are they currently interested in being in the type of relationship that you're looking for, e.g. if you want a FWB, are they interested in being FWB with someone? Do they talk openly and comfortably about romance? If they seem reserved and avoidant of the topic, it may mean that they're not fully ready for a relationship.

- ☐ Social Cues

    This one's a little bit of a no-brainer but, do they think of you favourably or, at least, not in a negative light? Are they willing to help you in terms of small favours? What about bigger favours? If you were to smile at them (non-creepily), will they smile back? The most amazing thing about human social behaviour is that so much can be learnt without a single word being spoken. Reading their body language is a great way to work out what they think of you.

☐ Relationship Aptitude

> Emotional availability is good, but it's not everything. Just because someone is ready to date, doesn't mean they'll be good at it. Observe their dating history and social media. If they have a history of negative relationships, you might want to take a step back. It doesn't necessarily mean it's their fault, but they might be having trouble maintaining a relationship at the moment.

☐ Personality Red Flags

> A wise old man once said, 'if a person doesn't use a special voice for animals and small children, they shouldn't be trusted'. And that wise old man was me. Okay, there's not much basis to that statement but the point is that a person's treatment to vulnerable groups says a lot about them as a person. Are they outspoken about various social issues (e.g. environment, wellbeing of others)? Do they react in a civil manner when someone makes a mistake? Are they physically violent when emotional? Relationships require you to be vulnerable, so it's important the person doesn't take advantage of that. For more information on abuse, go to part 8, The Silent Hand.

Are You Playing this Game on High Difficulty? (LGBT)

In the dating pool, things aren't always equal. Those that are in the LGBT community may find an increased difficulty in pursuit. That's because the majority of the population are cishet people interested in finding other cishet people. So what can you do? First of all, never give up! Though it may be hard, it's not impossible. LGBT people do exist after all – they can be simply hidden behind a shroud of heteronormativity. It's not that you can't play the game; you just have to play the game with more care. Here are some tips of pursuit when you're LGBT.

Assess their sexual orientation – lots of queer folks agree the most painful thing in the world is falling for someone that is straight. Or even worse, being stuck in a pur-gay-tory where you're not sure what their sexuality is. It's very daunting to straight up ask them, so it's more ideal to find out via social cues. Firstly, look at their friendship circle. Although not always the case, many LGBT people tend to have other LGBT people in their friendship circles. Sometimes, this can happen unintentionally, as I have seen this happen with my friend's old primary school group. As they approached high school, one of them came out, and gradually they all did. There's no formal explanation to this phenomenon but many people think it might be because we all subconsciously connect to people that are similar to us.

Next, look at their day-to-day life. Do they take an interest in things that belong to queer culture? This may include singers, actors and films that are quite prominent in the LGBT community. Although traditionally there have been certain physical 'signs' to indicate one's sexuality, it is now considered rather inaccurate and stereotypical to base your assumption on those things only. In general, you can never be 100% sure what a person's sexuality is, even if they seem to meet all the criteria. The only way you can be certain is to ask.

Assessing their political standpoint - Identity politics are something that almost everyone would be exposed to in this day and age. If you're heterosexual but not cisgender, then you've got a unique problem to face. To ensure your success and SAFETY, it's important to find out the other person's view on identity politics. To assess that, you can bring up recent events in the news regarding transgender rights and gauge their response. If they seem to talk about transgender folks in a negative light, you need to immediately back off.

If you really want to, you can opt for dating apps. However, like any type of platform that allows you to interact with strangers online, you need to stay safe. Safety when online dating is something that needs to be addressed regardless of your sexuality. Moreover, most dating apps are designed for hook-ups, rather than committed relationships (of course, if you're aromantic and just want a sexual relationship that's great for you). Once in a while, people might get lucky, but the best way to meet someone is through networking in real life. Having a few queer friends in your circle is a great start. Then, each of them will have other queer friends and so on. When you have a solid network, there's bound to be someone who you like and likes you back.

LGBT people deserve to find love too, don't forget that. So, don't give up, and try your best!

The Chess Game of Flirting

"Flirting is like a game of chess ... one wrong move and you are married!"

That above quote is one you'll see circulating on social media, usually posted by baby boomers. I'm sad that Boomer Facebook humour has ruined the association of chess and flirting because it is honestly the best analogy out there.

Flirting is a strategy game for two people: you and the person you're interested in. And just like a game of chess, there's no single method of play. Each turn and move you make is going to be unique depending on the person and situation. Flirting is a very broad term defined as 'behaving as though sexually attracted to someone, but playfully rather than with serious intentions'. Notice the 'serious intentions' part. Flirting can be non-serious and have no strings attached. It is also perfect for the pursuit route because it serves as a way to gauge a person's interest in you without investing too much.

There's no single formula to flirting. You need to combine many different actions strategically in response to the other person. Flirting can come in many forms, each with different functions, just like chess pieces. If I jotted down every single way you can flirt, it would go on forever. This list is only there to give you some ideas. Eventually, you'll get to a point where flirting becomes natural and you won't be struggling. Trust me.

Conversation	❖ Pointed compliments
	❖ Initiating conversation with them
	❖ Asking about people they care about
	❖ Offering encouragement and support
	❖ Playful insults (I mean PLAYFUL)
	❖ Laugh at their jokes
Body language	❖ Unfolded arms
	❖ General open posture
	❖ Eye contact
	❖ Smiling when talking
	❖ Crossing/uncrossing legs (girls)
	❖ Leaning in
	❖ Looking excited when you see them
Actions	❖ Brushing past them subtly
	❖ Playfully touching their arm
	❖ Hugs (if they're consensual)
	❖ Tucking a piece of hair back for them

Actions (cont'd)	❖	Winking
	❖	Wearing cologne/perfume
Miscellaneous	❖	Remembering small details about them
	❖	Taking time out to spend with them
	❖	Getting them small gifts
	❖	Doing small favours for them

While you play your moves, the other person is playing theirs too. However, there's three possible ways to play back: offensive, defensive and neutral. What we would want is offensive play from them, where they use moves on you as well. This signifies mutual interest. On the other hand, the person may be aware that you're flirting but aren't interested. They would play defensively by blocking out your advances covertly. If you can feel that happening, it's best to pull away. Finally, the person might just be really oblivious and not know you've initiated a game of chess. Their rebuffs to your advances may most likely not be hostile, but they might not take you anywhere. For situations like this, it is up to you whether or not you want to continue trying.

So you've got the foundations of the game down, let's amp it up and learn some more practical skills.

Strategies

This is the most practical this book's going to get. Loaded in this subsection are things you can whip out in the battlefield. But before that, here are some game rules.

The Do's and Don'ts of Going After Someone
Do!

- ❖ Be confident in yourself. You might think you're being someone more appealing but that will wear thin over time.

- ❖ Have a sense of humour. Flirting is supposed to be fun! Being light-hearted also helps cushion rejection of advancements.

- ❖ Get a friend to act as your wingman. Preferably, someone that has read this book and can read social cues.

- ❖ Plan as you go. Flirting is a real-time board game, so make moves as deemed fit at the given time.

Don't!

- ❖ Come on too strong. Remember, the definition of flirting says no 'serious intentions'. It's better to look light-hearted than desperate you know?

- ❖ Keep trying after they've said no. This will very quickly turn into harassment if you don't!

- ❖ Laugh at every single thing they say. Sure, laughing at someone's joke is a form of flirting, but there's a limit.

- ❖ Maintain unbroken eye contact. Same with above, it'll just get a little creepy eventually.

101 Pickup lines

There's something I need to say before you go on. Way too many people misuse pickup lines, and that's why they don't bloody work. They think that they're like a magic spell that will immediately enchant someone at the bar. No! Don't expect to get a positive reaction by going to someone and delivering one of these. The notion of the pickup line has become so packaged and artificial that we're better off seeing them as romantically-themed one-liner jokes. Besides, I'm sure your crush has already heard of 90% of these off the Internet and doesn't want to hear the rest.

So how would you use these? Be ironic and bond with your crush by discussing pickup lines. Maybe you two can talk about how sexist they are or something. Or, you can go even go full Meta and 'roleplay' using them. This is a very good strategy because fun fact, roleplay is a powerful psychological tool (more psychological tools will be available later in this chapter). Even from a young age, you've seen children playing make-believe. Roleplaying serves as a way to do things and take on identities without investing in them. It serves as a shield for the self. Think roleplaying video games. Think roleplaying in the sexual way. You see what I'm getting at? Also, if your crush willingly 'roleplays' flirting with you in the first place then congratulations, there's a pretty big chance they want that to be real. Note: Some of these may have slightly crude and stereotyping undertones. Others are just dumb.

1. Are you French because Eiffel for you.

2. Is that a mirror in your pocket? Cause I can see myself in your pants!

3. Are you religious? Cause you're the answer to all my prayers.

4. Hey, tie your shoes! I don't want you falling for anyone else.

5. You must be Jamaican, because Jamaican me crazy.

6. What has 36 teeth and holds back the Incredible Hulk? My zipper.

7. Somebody call the cops, because it's got to be illegal to look that good!

8. I must be a snowflake, because I've fallen for you.

9. I know you're busy today, but can you add me to your to-do list?

10. If you were a steak, you would be well done.

11. Hello, I'm a thief, and I'm here to steal your heart.

12. Are you cake? Cause I want a piece of that.

13. My love for you is like diarrhoea, I just can't hold it in.

14. Are you lost ma'am? Because heaven is a long way from here.

15. There is something wrong with my cell phone. It doesn't have

your number in it.

16. If you were a library book, I would check you out.

17. Are you a cat? Cause I'm feline a connection between us

18. If I were to ask you out on a date, would your answer be the same as the answer to this question?

19. If nothing lasts forever, will you be my nothing?

20. I'm new in town. Could you give me directions to your apartment?

21. I must be in a museum, because you are truly a work of art.

22. You spend so much time in my mind, I should charge you rent.

23. My lips are like skittles. Wanna taste the rainbow?

24. Well, here I am. What were your other two wishes?

25. Are you from Tennessee? Because you're the only 10 I see!

26. Are you a beaver? Cause daaaaaaaaam!

27. Life without you is like a broken pencil ... pointless.

28. Do you want to see a picture of a beautiful person? (hold up a mirror)

29. Is your body from McDonald's? Cause I'm lovin' it!

30. Even if there wasn't gravity on earth, I'd still fall for you.

31. Roses are red, violets are blue, how would you like it if I came home with you?

32. I wish I were cross-eyed so I could see you twice

33. We're not socks. But I think we'd make a great pair.

34. Your lips look so lonely ... would they like to meet mine?

35. Are you a parking ticket? Cause you've got fine written all over you.

36. Thank god I'm wearing gloves because you are too hot to handle.

37. If a fat man puts you in a bag at night don't worry, I told Santa I wanted you for Christmas.

38. I'm no photographer, but I can picture us together.

39. Do your legs hurt from running through my dreams all night?

40. Pinch me, you're so fine I must be dreaming.

41. If you were a chicken, you'd be im-peck-able.

42. How much does a polar beat weigh? Enough to break the ice!

43. Are you a 90 degree angle? Cause you are looking right!

44. Nice to meet you, I'm (your name) and you are ... gorgeous!

45. If I were a transplant surgeon, I'd give you my heart.

46. Are you Israeli? Cause you Israeli hot.

47. On a scale from 1 to 10, you're a 9 ... And I'm the 1 you need.

48. Did it hurt when you fell from heaven?

49. If I could rearrange the alphabet, I would put U and I together.

50. Remember me? Oh, that's right. I've only met you in my dreams.

51. Is your name Google? Because you've got everything I'm searching for.

52. Your hand looks heavy. Here, let me hold it for you.

53. I've been wondering, do your lips taste as good as they look.

54. Are you from Starbucks? Cause I like you a latte.

55. Are you a banana? Cause I find you a-peeling.

56. Do you like vegetables? Cause I love you from my head tomatoes.

57. Have you been to the doctor's lately? Cause I think you're lacking some vitamin me.

58. Do you generate electricity with water through the process of hydro power? Because dammmm.

59. Do you like science? Cause I've got my ion you.

60. Are you my appendix? Because I don't understand how you

work but this feeling in my stomach makes me want to take you out.

61. Do you like sales? Because if you're looking for a good one, clothing is 100% off at my place.

62. I know this is going to sound cheesy, but I think you're the gratest.

63. If you were a triangle, you'd be acute one.

64. Does your left eye hurt? Because you've been looking right all day.

65. My feet are getting cold ... because you've knocked my socks off.

66. Wow, when God made you he was showing off.

67. If beauty were time, you'd be eternity.

68. Is your name Wi-fi? Because I'm really feeling a connection.

69. If looks could kill, you'd be a weapon of mass destruction.

70. Do you have a tan, or do you always look this hot?

71. Can I follow you home? Cause my parents always told me to follow my dreams.

72. If I were a cat, I'd spend all 9 lives with you.

73. Are you a camera? Because every time I look at you, I smile.

74. Are you from Japan? Cause I'm trying to get in Japanties.

75. If you were a fruit you'd be a fineapple.

76. I'll give you a kiss. If you don't like it, you can return it.

77. Did you swallow a magnet? Cause you're attractive.

78. Are you from China? Because I'm China get your number.

79. Do you have a name, or can I call you mine?

80. Are you craving Pizza? Because I'd love to get a pizz-a you.

81. Wouldn't we look cute on a wedding cake together?

82. Would you grab my arm so I can tell my friends I've been touched by an angel?

83. Kiss me if I'm wrong, but dinosaurs still exist, right?

84. Is your dad a terrorist? Because you are the bomb.

85. You must be a ninja, because you snuck into my heart

86. Can you pinch me? Because you're so fine I must be dreaming.

87. I may not be a genie, but I can make all your wishes come true!

88. Are you Australian? Because you meet all of my koala-fications.

89. I'm not drunk, I'm just intoxicated by you.

90. If I followed you home, would you keep me?

91. If you were words on a page, you'd be fine print.

92. Are you a keyboard? Because you are my type.

93. There is something wrong with my phone. Could you call it for me to see if it rings?

94. I've seem to have lost my number, can I have yours?

95. If I had a garden, I'd put your tulips and my tulips together

96. Did you hear of the new disease called beautiful? I think you're infected.

97. I thought Happiness starts with H. But why does mine starts with U?

98. If you were a vegetable, you'd be a cutecumber.

99. You know what you would really look beautiful in? My arms.

100. You must be a magician, because every time I look at you, everyone else disappears.

101. You're like a dictionary ... you add meaning to my life.

I hope you're able to get through all of them without cringing too much. Anyway, moving on.

101 Icebreakers

Icebreakers can be used in a more normal context as opposed to pickup lines. That's because they don't have a direct, purposeful energy. Icebreakers are honestly very neutral and don't have any romantic connotations in them. This is great because if you flirt using an icebreaker, it serves as a safety net in case the other person isn't interested in you. It's better to have a friend than an awkward acquaintance you have to sit next to every Chemistry lesson. Icebreakers belong to the 'conversation' section of flirting strategies as they help you to get to know them better.

1. Where did you grow up?
2. Do you have any pets?
3. Do you have any siblings?
4. Do you know what your name means?
5. What type of phone do you have?
6. What did you do this past weekend?
7. What are your plans for this weekend?
8. What do you like to do in your spare time?
9. What is the first thing you do when you wake up?
10. What is the last thing you do before you go to sleep?
11. What is your middle name?

12. What was the last thing you purchased?

13. What is your favourite holiday?

14. What is your favourite day of the week?

15. If you could meet anyone in history, who would it be?

16. What do you like to do to relax?

17. Are you a saver or a spender?

18. Do you play any instruments?

19. What was your favourite children's book?

20. What is your first childhood memory?

21. What kind of kid were you (e.g. spoiled, rebellious, well-behaved, quiet, obnoxious...)?

22. What is one thing you miss about being a kid?

23. What did you want to grow up to be when you were younger?

24. Where did (do) you go to primary/high school?

25. What was (is) your favourite subject?

26. What was (is) your least favourite subject?

27. What's the first thing you do after school/work?

28. Were you the class clown or teacher's pet?

29. What do you do for a living?

30. What is your dream job?

31. If you had $10 million, would you still be working/going to school?

32. What was your least favourite job that you've ever had?

33. What is something that you have gotten in trouble for at school/work?

34. What is the first think you notice about a guy or girl?

35. Have you ever been in love?

36. Do you believe in soul mates?

37. What are your turn offs?

38. Do you believe in love at first sight?

39. Do you prefer short hair or long hair on a guy/girl?

40. What do you look for in a guy/girl?

41. Who was the last person you called?

42. Would you rather be rich and never find true love or be poor and find true love?

43. Who is your favourite athlete?

44. How often do you exercise?

45. What is your favourite sports team?

46. Do you play any sports?

47. Where was the last place you went on vacation?

48. Where do you plan on going for your next vacation?

49. If you could live anywhere in the world, where would it be?

50. What countries have you travelled to?

51. What was your worst vacation experience?

52. What is your favourite drink?

53. What is your favourite food?

54. What is your favourite meal of the day?

55. Are there any foods that you dislike or won't eat?

56. Are there any foods that you would like to try?

57. What is your favourite restaurant?

58. What is your favourite pizza topping?

59. What is your favourite ice cream flavour?

60. What did you have for dinner last night?

61. What is the signature dish that you cook?

62. Who is your favourite actor?

63. What is your favourite movie of all time?

64. What was the worst movie you've ever seen?

65. What is your favourite TV show?

66. What was the last movie you've seen?

67. What type of music do you like to listen to?

68. Who is your favourite music artist?

69. What was the last book you read?

70. Who do you look up to?

71. Where do you see yourself 5 years from now?

72. What are you scared of?

73. What is the best piece of advice you've received?

74. What do your parents do for a living?

75. What is your biggest regret?

76. What is your most embarrassing moment?

77. What is the craziest thing you've ever done?

78. What are some of your short-term goals?

79. What are some of your long-term goals?

80. Do you sleep with a stuffed animal?

81. Tell me about your first car.

82. Do you drink coffee or tea?

83. If you could have any super power, what would it be?

84. If you could only eat one dessert forever, what will it be?

85. Do you believe in luck?

86. Do you play video games?

87. Do you believe people are inherently good?

88. How often do you shower?

89. What is your favourite board game?

90. What is your favourite charity?

91. Have you ever gotten a speeding ticket?

92. Do you prefer cats or dogs?

93. Would you prefer to live in the city or a rural area?

94. What is your favourite season?

95. Do you speak any other languages?

96. Have you ever cried because you were so happy?

97. What is the best thing that happened to you during the past week?

98. What is the worst thing that happened to you during the past week?

99. Do you sing in the shower?

100. What is the most valuable thing that you own?

101. What would you do if you only had 24 hours left to live?

The 20-question method

Yes, this is the 20-question method that a bunch of 14-year-olds came up with on Tumblr. But so what? The point isn't in the actual strategy itself, but the framework it provides for flirting. Essentially, how this method works is: you make them play a game of 20-questions (which is already an icebreaker in itself) and work closer and closer to their romantic status. What makes this great is that as the game is turn-based, there are many different steps for you to backtrack in case things aren't going well. Unfortunately, the original post has been buried under years and years of new Tumblr content, so I would like to apologise for being unable to trace the author. If fate ever allows you to come across this book, let me salute you. Here's the best version I can create from memory. Let's get into it.

1. Tell the person you want to play 20-questions as an icebreaker/boredom buster.

2. If they ask questions that are creepy, you know that's a red flag.

3. Start off easy with small-talk questions, then work up to questions with more thought.

4. While you do this, take note of their interests etc.

5. Past the tenth question, if things seem alright, move on to a more romantic direction.

6. Ask questions like, "what type of things do you find attractive in a person?"

7. Gauge their reactions to romantic questions. If they're clearly unengaged, then that's a sign.

8. At any given time, if you feel like the outcome is undesirable, abort plan and play normally.

9. See if they ask you questions back. Answer strategically, but do not lie.

10. If you think things are going well, your final question will be "would you ever consider going out with me?" If they say no, you can laugh it off and say it's just a game. If they say yes, then congrats!

Despite this being a text post right out of a Tumblr blog in 2010, it's pretty good. You can even apply this strategy to other real-world instances. When it comes to reaching an end goal, it's important to see them as separate steps, each with a fall-back in case of unexpected things. It's much better to have a plan than to just dive in, especially if this is your first try at it. Who knew kids on Tumblr could be so profound?

Five Sweet Brain Tricks

Ah yes, psychology is an amazing thing. The brain is the most complex machine known to man, so a study dedicated to it is going to bring some crazy discoveries. When it comes to intrapersonal interactions, psychology is going to be involved because it represents the invisible forces that fuel the 'thought machines' in our heads. Even this far into the book, you've already encountered a lot of psychology. But if you're really keen on harnessing this power properly, here are a few you can try.

The power of psychology is like fire. It's really powerful and useful but without proper knowledge of its procedures, you can easily burn yourself. So I hope that you'll use them to be a more attractive person, or to try and get someone, but not to cause harm.

Pavlov's Conditioning (Ivan Pavlov)

So essentially, this one is all about conditioning. When you're talking or interacting with your crush, do something else that they like. It doesn't have to be very obvious stuff. Maybe just buy them food they like, or talk to them about a topic they like. You might think this is basic but it will surprise you how effective it is. It will be very beneficial for your crush to associate you with positive things.

Spontaneous Trait Transference (Skowronski, Carlston, Mae, and Crawford)
What this means is that people will associate the adjectives you use about other people with your personality. I know it sounds unreal, but studies have found that people actually saw traits in others based on *their* adjectives for others, even if it's not accurate. If you were to compliment another person on their kindness in front of your crush often, the chances are that they will feel that you are kind.

Pratfall Effect (Elliot Aronson)
Did you know that occasionally making mistakes and being clumsy makes you more attractive?! You might think this is a contradictory point to the psychology behind infatuations, right? When you're infatuated with someone, you perceive them as perfect and therefore obsess over them. But the Pratfall effect works because flaws make someone seem more vulnerable and relatable. And these two traits may be part of someone's 'infatuation lenses', right? If you don't get what I mean that's ok. Of course, this phenomenon has limitations. You can't just screw up everything all the time to the point that it frustrates your crush. Oh, and you also have to start off on good terms with them first for it to work.

Self-Verification Theory (William Swann)

Everyone's got a personal brand. The problem is that everyone's also got their own view of said brand. A person feels happiest and most validated when others can perceive them as the way they want to be. We all like our views and opinions to be confirmed by others after all. This can be trivial things like their hobbies and talents, or deeper things like their self-image. Studies show that people with positive self-views like people that have positive views of them (no-brainer), while people that think negatively of themselves like critics.

Chameleon Effect (John Bargh)

Naturally, when two people get closer, they start to mimic each other. This is due to the increased physical and emotional intimacy between them. Each person's identities start to overlap and that's where the Chameleon Effect happens. However, you can also do this consciously to speed up the process. Mimicking the person you want to attract will make them like you more. This can be in terms of body language, gestures and facial expressions.

Friendship, Just the Perfect Blend-Ship!

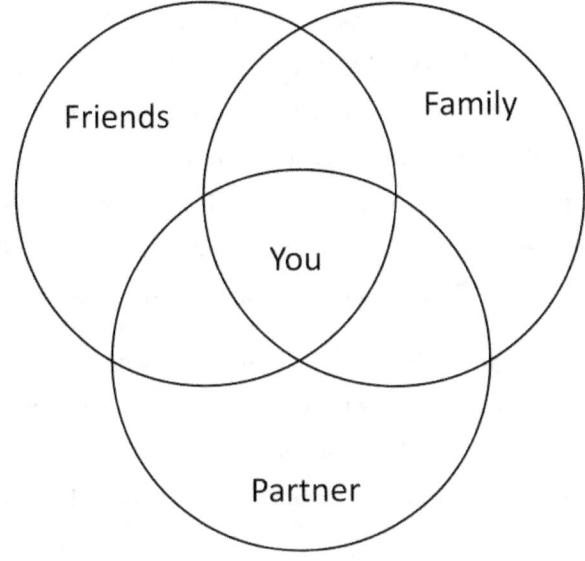

When we think of personal circles, we've got three main ones: family, friends and romance. But did you know that all of these are and should be interconnected? They should all interact with each other and some might even overlap. With that being said, many young people (and I mean many) find that they have problems with their friendship circle after a romance circle is introduced. For the sake of the target demographic of this, I'm going to focus on the interactions between the friend and romance. You see, the family/romance overlap only happens a little later on in life when relationships get more serious.

It's important to keep both circles healthy. Tragedy always strikes when there's an imbalance. You need to make sure you have strong, supportive friends that only want the best for you. And your partner also needs to understand that you need a balance. Your friends are going to react in two possible ways when you tell them about your latest romantic target. They're either going to squeal/high-five you or they're not going to react much, maybe verbally dry-text you. So which reaction means that you have good, real supportive friends? Go and take a guess and I'll tell you the answer in the next paragraph.

It's a trick question. Both of those reactions can mean you have good/bad friends. That's why the judgement is up to you. I love tables so here's one I put together to summarise what the possible situations can be. The two variables are your friend's nature and your target's nature.

	Your target's trash	**Your target's good**
Your friends are trash	Will encourage you due to spite/poor judgement	Will discourage you due to jealousy/spite
Your friends are good	Will discourage you due to awareness of toxicity	Will encourage you due to awareness of benefits

See?! Reaction ≠ quality of relationship. So what can you do? First of all, increase your sample space. You may have a few trash friends, but that doesn't mean that your entire friendship circle is trash (if it is, then you'll seriously need to find new friends and start over, damn). Watch how people talk. Yes, even though both good and bad friends will display encouragement and discouragement, the way they do it will differ. It's clearer to see it in their criticism than their praise. A bad friend's arguments can get quite low, to the point where it starts to be about YOU instead of the other person. A good friend's criticism of your target will focus on how they will harm your personal growth.

Be observant about how your friends act around you and your target. If you're already dating and your friends seem to get in the way a lot, be careful. This can be physically, as in using body language and blocking between you and your partner, or disrupting plans. It can also be verbal, which like above, refers to put downs that discourage the relationship. A friend with good faith in their intervention will almost always talk to you first and explain what's going on. A bad friend's intervention is commonly fuelled by bitterness or even jealousy.

In case you seriously don't know what's happening between your friends and your partner, you shouldn't rely just on your instincts. They will be clouded when you're in love, as I mentioned a few chapters before. Even though it's hard, the only way you can properly secure circles is to speak up. You may end up losing your partner or your friend but hey, in order to weed a garden, you need to rip the weed out by its roots.

I've witnessed many clashes between friendship and romance in my high school life. There are some experiences that I've witnessed as a friend myself, other times I was the one dealing with ambiguous friends. Perhaps the most tragic thing that ever happened to me was when I got together with someone that was clearly manipulative. Apparently, she was enemies with one of my close friends, and her agenda was to date me to spite them. My friends held their tongues, maybe because they thought that I would be upset if they tried to tell me what was up. At the same time, I was stupid and failed to observe the situation - the situation being that the person I dated was literally bullying my friend. As soon as I got dumped, everything became clear. So, never again, I told myself, would I let that happen. I've also been on the flip side, where I became a devil's advocate for my friend because I could clearly see the dire consequences of their relationship but they couldn't.

Part 5

It Takes a Spark

There's a nice fluffy feeling in your heart that's been flickering for a few days now. In fact, you can feel your own life revolving around that feeling. It's just tiny things, like your heart throbbing at the sight of their 'online' icon, or a shortness of breath at the scent of their perfume. Right now, your heart is a powder keg.

And all it takes is a spark.

The Leap

Flirting is all fun and games because there's no strings attached to it. You can do it to multiple people at the same time too. But eventually, there'll be someone, or some people, where you feel the flirting is quickly evolving into something else. For the sake of easy reading in this chapter, I'll assume that you plan to date <u>mutually exclusively</u>, and are asking someone to go on a date with you for the first time.

What does that mean? Mutual exclusion (ME) in dating means that you and the other person are only actively seeing (or have agreed to, there's always cheating) each other romantically. On the flip side, if you and the person are mutually inclusive (MI), it means both of you are free to go on dates and flirt with other people as well. This type of openness has the similar unrestricted vibes that flirting has, so people who don't want to take a big leap will do that. I personally am an ME dater, so I don't feel credible enough to talk about how dating would work for the other method.

Just to make things even more confusing, mutual exclusion also is different from a boyfriend/girlfriend relationship. Mutual exclusion means you and the other person are seeing each other, but you are both still CONSIDERING. That means both can deem the other unfit and walk away with (almost) no strings attached. You don't even need to call it a 'break-up' when that happens, you can just go and try another person in an ME relationship. So in reality, what really differs between ME and MI is that you either consider one person at a time or you consider multiple people at once. An MI can end with you choosing the best person, or dating multiple people, if you're polyamorous.

So anyway, the leap. Dates typically include an event. You can't just ask someone to go into an ME relationship randomly over text. When you're getting into a serious relationship, you can maybe ask without an event, but let's cross the bridge when we get there, okay?

Here's a good breathing exercise to ease the nerves:

Square Breathing

1. Slowly exhale, getting all the oxygen out of your lungs. Focus on this intention and be conscious of what you're doing.

2. Inhale slowly and deeply through your nose to the count of four slowly.

3. Hold your breath for another slow count of four.

4. Exhale through your mouth for the count of four. Be conscious of the feeling of the air leaving your lungs.

5. Hold your breath for the same slow count of four before repeating this process.

This is a run-down of how to ask someone out:

1. Get to know said person.
2. Think of an event.
3. Find a good time to strike up conversation.
4. Ask them to go on a date.
5. If successful, prep for the date and take second steps.
6. If unsuccessful, deal with the rejection.

Contact the person that you want to go on a date with. Although many old-timey people shun the use of technology when asking such a serious request, sometimes it's inevitable. I've used texts to plan first dates myself. So I ask that no matter how you do it, just make sure you're sincere and not casual. Don't make it sound like a 'by the way' segue after chatting about football. Although it's conventional for your first date to be just the two of you, it's common for younger people to make it a group event to make it less awkward. For adults, doing this as a first date is very bad, but teens and tweens get a pass for it. However, with more people involved there are more liabilities to manage. Make sure the friends that are going on the 'date' with you are RELIABLE. Remember the previous section. You need to be careful with who you invite and be vigilant on how they act.

Think of an idea for a first date. It doesn't have to be elaborate because at this point you two most likely aren't invested enough into each other emotionally to know specifics for a person (so no IKEA shopping on the first date). Despite that, you should also be able to take into consideration the other person's preferences. A date revolving around food is almost likely to appeal to everyone. But if you know that they're especially interested in a particular band that you would also be happy seeing, you can get tickets. It's a bonus if the date includes BOTH a meal and an activity, but that's only if time and money allows.

Really stuck on date ideas? Fear not, I've got a list of some good first dates people do, both traditional and fun:

1. Cafe
2. Lunch
3. Dinner
4. Laser tag
5. Karaoke
6. Cooking
7. Ice cream date
8. Food festival/street fair
9. Theme park
10. Beach
11. Pool
12. Hiking
13. Sporting events
14. Zoo
15. Skate park
16. Painting
17. Bowling
21. Museum
22. Ice-skating
23. Volunteering
24. Gym
25. A walk
26. Golf
27. Trampoline park
28. Picnic
29. Dog/cat café
30. Haunted house
31. Yoga
32. Comedy show
33. Bookstore
34. Arcade
35. Botanical garden
36. Planetarium
37. Running

18. Trivia night

19. Dance class

20. Board games/pool

38. Roller skating/skateboarding

39. Aquarium

40. Rock climbing

Apart from this list, there are many other great activities that are a great for dates. However, there are a few that shouldn't be done for a *first* date. The first date is vital for getting to know a person 'out of hours, that is, away from the place you've most likely met them (school, work etc.) where we are artificially constructed most of the time. It also allows you to see them better, relaxed and not in a uniform.

So here are some dates that you should stay clear from at first and reserve for later.

1. **Cinema** - you're both fixated on a movie, so you can't talk and get to know them. It's also really dark so you can't see what they're doing. It can get awkward on a first date especially when you don't know if you can touch them or not.

2. **Double date** - hell no. Double dates can be very fun, don't get me wrong, but not on the first date. This is different from having other friends around because the romantic tension is higher. It puts pressure on your date especially if the other couple is already quite stable.

3. **Family event** - meeting extended family is very crucial but it requires so much foundation that it's probably not even a suitable date for an ME relationship in the first place. Perhaps do this when you're in a serious relationship.

4. **'Come over and chill'** - a date where you invite the other person to your house is not a 'date'. In fact, it just lets them know you're too lazy to think of anything to do. A person's house is sacred and you only let someone you're dating go in after a few dates. Unless it's just a hook-up.

5. **Concert/club** - These are places where you will most likely meet someone, so don't take a date there. Besides, these places are loud and full of people, so good luck getting to know the other person over the sound of rowdy people.

The Baby Steps of Baby Steps

Suppose your crush has actually said yes to your proposal. Before we continue, give yourself a pat on the back for this achievement. Alright, so plans are made, but the next important thing is the etiquette surrounding a first date. Don't worry; I'm not going to be educating you on out-dated heteronormative things. No, I'm giving out etiquette that is relevant and applicable to everyone in the twenty-first century.

1. **Dress for the occasion** - no need to go out of your comfort zone, but you probably shouldn't put on your grey hoodie if you're going to the beach.

2. **Be yourself** - especially during the parts where you reveal things about yourself, never pretend to be someone else. Eventually lies will snowball and explode.

3. **Be punctual** - no one likes waiting anxiously for someone that they're supposed to be on a first date with. I was late for a first date and my date ended up getting hit on by an old man.

4. **Don't get intoxicated** - if your first date includes alcohol, feel free to have some. It can help ease your nerves. But don't drink so much that you embarrass yourself.

5. **Engage in conversation** - I know it seems obvious, but you need to be engaging. Ask them interesting questions, flirt a little, and talk about yourself. Don't overdo small talk and don't overshare.

6. **Get off your phone** - this is a tip you certainly won't see in vintage dating pamphlets, but you'll need it. Please for the love of God look at your date instead. Extra shitty if what you're looking at is Tinder.

7. **Chill out** - remember dates are supposed to be fun. If anything undesirable happens, keep your cool and don't make a big deal out of it. This goes with bills, distractions and your actual date.

8. **Get external help** - if you really need to, you can get one of your friends to wingman you, as long as they're just on standby and not interrupting your date (more on that in part 10).

9. **Don't dig up the past** - don't mention your exes on the first date. You're supposed to be focusing on the present, not the past.

10. **Be polite** - it doesn't matter what gender you are. You can hold the door open. You can pull out their chair. Say thank you to staff who do things for you. Go outside if you receive a phone call.

Limits and Pacing

Different people have different expectations for how romance paces for them. There are people that don't hold hands until the third date, and there are also people that have sex on the first date. Both you and the other person need to have a conversation. If you don't, there can be consequences ranging from not having a second date to one of you committing sexual assault. Communication is very important and assumptions never help anyone. I understand it might feel weird to ask about this on dates but trust me, developing good communication habits early on will be VERY beneficial for the future.

Here's some ways you can talk about pacing without it being awkward:

- ❖ "How are you feeling about us? Do you feel comfortable?"
- ❖ "What's on your mind for the next date?"
- ❖ "Can you let me know if you think we're advancing too fast?"

The skill of understanding your partner's limits will help you a lot in almost all areas of a relationship, including sex and moving in together. When you both share what you're willing and not willing to do, a compromise can be made where both of you can meet in the middle. Sounds great.

Dating from the Same School?

I'm assuming here that my demographic are teens, so listen up. As a teen, your world is quite limited. Think of high school as a fish tank, then university is an aquarium and the work world is the whole ocean. As you progress in life, there are less barriers and a bigger playing space. When you're a teenager in high school, most of your time is spent with the same bunch of people: your peers. To be honest with you, your options for dating are severely limited. Some people are bolder and extend out of their school via an online networking of friends, but most feel more comfortable and find it relatively easier to just date their class mates (high school sweethearts are common). There's no right way to find a date in high school, so I've prepared a pros and cons for both. Do what you want, and what you can. Oh, and these tables can kind of work too if you're in university, so there's that.

Dating Within the School/Campus

Pros	Cons
❖ You get to see them more often.	❖ You're going to be stuck seeing them everywhere when you break-up.
❖ Easier to deal with things in face-to-face conversation.	❖ Limited dating options.
❖ Your circle and theirs will overlap.	❖ Everyone at school will be nosier.
❖ Can easily provide support at school.	❖ Your grades could be affected.
❖ You get an additional companion during lunch.	❖ Distance can be difficult to deal with (after graduation).
❖ Engage in school-activities with them.	

Dating Outside of School/Campus

Pros	Cons
❖ It's more special every time you see them.	❖ It's more inconvenient to plan outings.
❖ There are more possible options.	❖ Harder to provide support for them.
❖ More mentally prepared for distance.	❖ Worrying that your partner's cheating.
❖ You can make a new friend circle outside school.	❖ Often restricted to virtual communication.
❖ You can experience the campus life of another school.	❖ You might feel lonely when surrounded by couples at school.
❖ Having a life away from your partner.	

I personally advocate for dating outside of school. It's just simply too restricting for you to look at the same 300 people for five years (if you're only attracted to one gender, then half of that). But either way it's up to you.

Taking the L

Yes, asking someone out requires them to answer. And there's two ways for them to - and one of them hurts a lot. Rejection at any point of a relationship hurts, because they all require you to destroy something you've made. And the longer you've worked on it, the more it will hurt. But don't worry, rejection is part of life. It's not the end of the world if someone doesn't want to go out with you. Don't feel angry if they say no even if it seemed like you two were getting on well with all the flirting and they were giving you very welcoming signs.

You must remember this: **no one owes you feelings**. They have the right to say no and you have to respect that. Maybe they're not ready, or maybe you've misread their signs. Either way, you should never, ever pressure them after they say no! If you truly like them, you should respect them as a person that has their own feelings and beliefs. Also, the friend zone is a funny relationship joke for prepubescent boys but beyond that, you should know there's no such thing. That's because the friend zone assumes that a person must owe the other sex based on a loyalty card of kindness. "I was nice to you eight times! The ninth time should give me free sex!" Just like a date, you never, ever 'owe' anyone sex, regardless of what they've done for you.

You'll of course feel sad that you've been rejected. But just because that person doesn't owe you feelings, doesn't mean you don't deserve love. Use the forget route to be more efficient with recovering emotionally. Relationships, let alone dates, aren't easy to coordinate. There are many different conditions that need to be met just right for a spark to ignite. There are people out there that keep liking each other, but all at different times. Therefore, while they've both felt attraction for each other, the timing was so poor that the feelings were never reciprocated. Stuff like this can happen. But you need to be opportunistic, because you miss 100% of the shots you don't shoot. And I have faith in you, dear reader. I know that one day you'll wake up and agree with me. When that happens, read on to the next chapter.

Part 6

A Free Shot of Oxytocin

You've had your first date, and it was great. You seem to have the prospect of a second date. But hold up a sec here, let's change gears and talk about brain stuff! After all, what's making you feel all dizzy when you kiss? What's imprinting the images of that certain someone in your head at night, long after you've said goodbye to them? Read on and you'll find out!

Hormones, Our Little Workers

These cute little chemicals in our brain do so much more than you think, and some of them affect our emotions. You've probably heard of the hormones that can make us happy, like serotonin, dopamine and endorphin.

But what about oxytocin? Oxytocin first does its job in the earliest form of love for a human – between child and mother. This hormone helps with labour, breastfeeding and bonding. But this hormone can also extend to relationships beyond that. Oxytocin is called the 'cuddle hormone' after all, and it literally does get released by affectionate contact and social bonding. Even playing with your dog can make your brain release some. Personally, I think oxytocin is the best hormone ever.

This chapter is going to be looking at the psychology behind romantic love, and how it affects different people. Yes, the information here will be more theory-based, but it's good to know what's happening to you so you're more confident in your own emotions.

Love Science

I've already talked about this in the first chapter, but love is so weird and amazing in the way that it's a unifying thing for humans, but at the same time is so versatile that no two people probably experience love the same way. I guess this is what makes love so beautiful, because you get to learn how another person's brain works and together you can create something amazing.

The Hormone's Game

Here's the 'love cocktail', or rather, how hormones come into play to create the complex physiological phenomenon of romantic love. Dr Helen Fisher at Rutgers suggests that it can be broken into three main categories:

Lust – sexual gratification	The need to reproduce is driven by our evolution of the brain. Frankly, if we don't have sex, we will die out. So of course, sex hormones play a key part. Testosterone and oestrogen increases libido in both genders.
Attraction – reward behaviour	Relationships set off the reward pathways of the brain, which is why

love feels euphoric. Dopamine is quite well-known for rewarding behaviour, but did you know that adrenaline also contributes? That's why you can feel so nervous when you're in love.

Attachment – social cordiality Our old friend oxytocin plays this part here. Again, oxytocin reigns supreme as it's responsible for bonding – a key ingredient in making intimate relationships that last. Vasopressin also helps out as well.

Everything seems nice and all, but as most things work in psychology, too much of a specific hormone will destroy you. That's why love isn't always nice and why some people get so consumed by it. I'm going to explain how the various hormones will contribute to common downfalls of love, but remember I'm not a professional so this information should be used for reference only.

Dopamine, the reward hormone, helps us enjoy things in life. But enjoyment can soon turn into addiction if dopamine is released very regularly in high amounts. Think recreational drugs. They work by overloading your brain with dopamine, which will feel very good, but overtime your brain will become numb to it and even develop a dependency. Then you'll find yourself needing to take higher and higher doses to achieve the same high. In terms of love, too much dopamine will cause us to become too emotionally dependent on our partners. This will make us unable to withdraw in case any obstacles occur. It will also hit you harder if they leave. Later on in this chapter, I'll talk about love withdrawal, and how it's dangerously similar to drug withdrawal.

So for oxytocin, too much of it can also be bad. The euphoria it provides can quickly evolve into recklessness. Have you seen people do stupid shit and then justify it with 'oh well, it's for love'. Uh, yeah sure. You're just high on oxytocin. If you've ever felt frustrated at how people have given up careers, family, mental health for others but don't even realise what they're doing, now you finally know why. To understand more on how relationships can take those things away from people, read up on red flags in Living the Honeymoon - part 7.

So anyway, play safe. Love is a nice cocktail of emotions but don't get too drunk on them.

The Five Love Languages

Gary Chapman's book *The Five Love Languages* has contributed a very interesting theory into psychology. There's not much official research to back it up, but many people do agree that he knows what it's talking about.

The book outlines that the five <u>love languages</u> are:

1. Words of Affirmation
2. Quality Time
3. Receiving Gifts
4. Acts of Service
5. Physical Touch

Everyone's way of demonstrating love will always revolve around these five, but what varies is what a person understands or 'speaks' mainly. When you're in a relationship, it's vital to know what language you speak, and what your partner speaks. To get that out of the way, get your partner to understand what the five languages are and then observe how you both interact. Most of the time, your language has always been there, you just didn't know what it was called.

Rosetta Stone

Here's a simple and short quiz for you and your partner to decide what your main love languages are. Remember, it's not that you only have one and is completely illiterate to the others. It just means you're more receptive to it.

To do this quiz, score yourself from 1–3 in each category for how much you value that thing. Then in the end, add the totals for each section. Your partner can then do it after you.

Section 1

- ❖ I love when my partner says, 'I love you'. ___
- ❖ I feel confident when my partner compliments my outfit. ___
- ❖ Conversing with my partner about anything is great. ___
- ❖ It's cute when my partner leaves me sticky notes around the house. ___
- ❖ I feel better when I talk to my partner about problems. ___

Section 2

- ❖ I like spending one-on-one time with my partner. ___
- ❖ Running any errand is better when my partner's there. ___
- ❖ I appreciate my partner's undivided attention. ___
- ❖ It's not the activity, but their presence that matters. ___
- ❖ I'm always looking forward to the next time I see them. ___

Section 3

- ❖ I love receiving gifts from my partner. ___
- ❖ I get very excited for gifts during holidays. ___
- ❖ A personalised gift is better than an expensive gift. ___

- ❖ It's important my partner remembers birthdays and anniversaries. ___

- ❖ Physical symbols of love are important to me. ___

Section 4

- ❖ It feels good coming home to chores already done. ___

- ❖ I feel loved when my partner helps me out physically. ___

- ❖ I love when my partner does things that I don't like to do. ___

- ❖ I appreciate my partner making hard decisions for me. ___

- ❖ Actions speak louder than words for me. ___

Section 5

- ❖ A hug from my partner feels the best. ___

- ❖ I hold hands with and kiss my partner regularly. ___

- ❖ I feel better when my partner physically comforts me. ___

- ❖ Being physically close to my partner is important. ___

- ❖ Physical contact makes me connected to my partner. ___

Add up the scores in all those sections and order them from highest to lowest. Although it's pretty obvious, each section translates like this:

Section 1: Words of Affirmation

Section 2: Quality Time

Section 3: Receiving Gifts

Section 4: Acts of Service

Section 5: Physical Touch

Let's see how these languages actually play in day-to-day life. Let's say that your main language is acts of service. So naturally, you'll be doing chores and work around the house for your partner because you love them and know they don't find washing dishes fun. But your partner's main language is actually words of affirmation. So you might feel frustrated that you're doing so much for them but they just see you as doing your part in the daily chores. At the same time, they're annoyed and don't know how much you care about them because you never talk or compliment them. Understanding literacy is very important. Just like if I was speaking Chinese and you were speaking French, we'd have no idea what on earth the other person was saying.

Makes and Breaks

A person's main love language will dictate what makes them feel the most valued, but also what hurts them the most. So be very careful and observant of yourself and your partner. The failure for a partner to understand your love language or vice versa can very easily break your relationship. More about how relationships fall apart will be seen in The Way the Cookie Crumbles, part 8.

	What is effective	**On the other hand...**
Words of affirmation	Unsolicited compliments feel amazing, and 'I Love You' packs a lot of meaning.	Insults and criticism hit very hard and aren't easily forgiven.
Quality time	Undivided attention gives a sense of respect and love, and so is lending an ear.	Distractions and postponed dates hurt a lot. So does the feeling of lack of listening.
Receiving gifts	Personalised gifts represent care and understanding.	Missed celebrations and last-minute gifts especially upset you.
Acts of service	Physical help in daily life speak much more volume than words do.	Laziness and broken commitments translate into lack of care.
Physical touch	Touch represents a high degree of concern, care and love.	Neglect and abuse are highly damaging to the relationship.

50 Ways to say I Love You

As you've learnt from the love languages, love can be displayed in many different ways. Here's 50 ways to demonstrate your love for your partner, categorised by love language for your convenience. Have fun showing your love!

Words of Affirmation

1. Say 'I Love You'
2. Get printable love notes off the internet
3. Frame the quote 'Home is wherever I am with you'
4. Text them good morning and goodnight
5. List 100 reasons why you love them
6. Leave notes in their car (if they have a car)
7. Say 'I love you today because ...' daily
8. Get a love story placemat
9. Make one of those 'I Love Us' books
10. Make them an A to Z list of what you love about them

Quality Time

1. Do a games night
2. Organise a couples date night quiz and interview (or Kahoot)
3. Make a couples bucket list
4. Play charades
5. Do a date night in a hammock
6. Sit back and let your partner decide a date
7. Organise a whole load of activities for your partner at home
8. Have a sleepover
9. Travel with your partner
10. Recreate past photos

Receiving Gifts

1. Give them an explosion box card
2. Get them a DIY t-shirt with your inside jokes on them
3. Turn your love story into a storybook
4. Make love notes into word magnets
5. Give them a gift that appeals to all five senses
6. Make them jewellery

7. Get them tickets to the game/concert they want to go to

8. Buy them a book that they've been wanting to get for a while

9. Name a star after them (I'm not kidding, you can do that)

10. Make a scrapbook of your photos

Acts of Service

1. Make them breakfast in bed

2. Do all the chores for the day

3. Get them a coupon book

4. Make them their favourite food

5. Do a spa date

6. Organise their room (if they let you)

7. Prepare dinner for them

8. Make a cup of tea

9. Draw them a bath with their favourite bath bomb

10. Make them laugh

Physical Touch

1. Give them a massage
2. Kiss and hold hands
3. Have consensual sex
4. Play spin the bottle
5. Play truth or dare
6. Give them a back rub
7. Cuddle on the couch
8. Take a shower/bath together
9. Sit side-by-side during a dinner date
10. Tickle them (that is only if they like getting tickled)

The Power of Touch

I would especially like to highlight the language of touch because it's very powerful. Of course, before I'd like to continue, I'd like to say that I do understand some people with sensory issues will hate physical contact, or some people just aren't touchy at all. If that's you, don't feel unnatural if this section doesn't apply to you much. It's okay to not want touch, even from your partner. They should understand what makes you feel comfortable and what makes your feel uncomfortable. Alright, now that I've got that out of the way, let's continue.

Touch is the first sense that we develop. For babies, it's the main sense they can use to comprehend affection. This carries on as we grow old, and there are many studies out there that reveal how touch greatly improves the bonding and trust between people. Therefore, many cultures incorporate it as a way of greeting and indicating friendliness. You probably hug and high-five people without knowing that you're actually reflecting physical actions of social bonding. Touch is very crucial for human development, and it's possible for someone to be 'touch-starved'.

Physical contact can become associated with negative situations as well. The strong emotional impact that touch gives mean many people feel much more violated and affected by negative touch than, for example, negative words. A more common word we might use in this instance is harassment. What people constitutes as harassments comes from many different factors, such as their perception on a person's gender, age, motivation, body part that they're touching and also physical boundaries. You may have one friend that feels totally fine with you kissing them on the cheek, and another that can't stand even a tap on the shoulder.

Unless you are touch-repulsed or have sensory issues (which, remember it's totally okay), touch is crucial for strengthening romantic relationships. There are studies that show partner contact reduces stress. The contact doesn't even have to be sexual – back rubs, hugs and hand holding all contribute to decreased blood pressure and improved mental state.

Touch Zones

Not all parts of the body give the same response when it comes to touch. You feel different things when your bro high-fives your hand or smacks your ass. A person's response to the touch can also vary in intensity. This links back to when I talked about how your friends all have different definitions of what feels like friendly bonding and what feels like it's starting to cross a line.

Making a map of your touch zones may feel weird, but it's one thing to know where you like to be touched, and another for you to be able to fully visualise it and relay that information to people that need to know. So here's how to make your personal 'touch map'. Your partner should also do one, so that you both understand boundaries, both sexual and non-sexual.

I've prepared a template below. You'll notice that there are four copies of the same template. That's because how you react to touch will be different based on circles. Most people are quite conservative with their touch when it comes to strangers, because there's no emotional connection and understanding yet. This can be imagined as an invisible force-field called the <u>touch barrier</u>. It's a primal safety mechanism to help us keep proximity with potentially dangerous individuals. It's important to understand this so that you can learn to respect it when first talking to a potential love interest, and then breaking the touch barrier when the time is right.

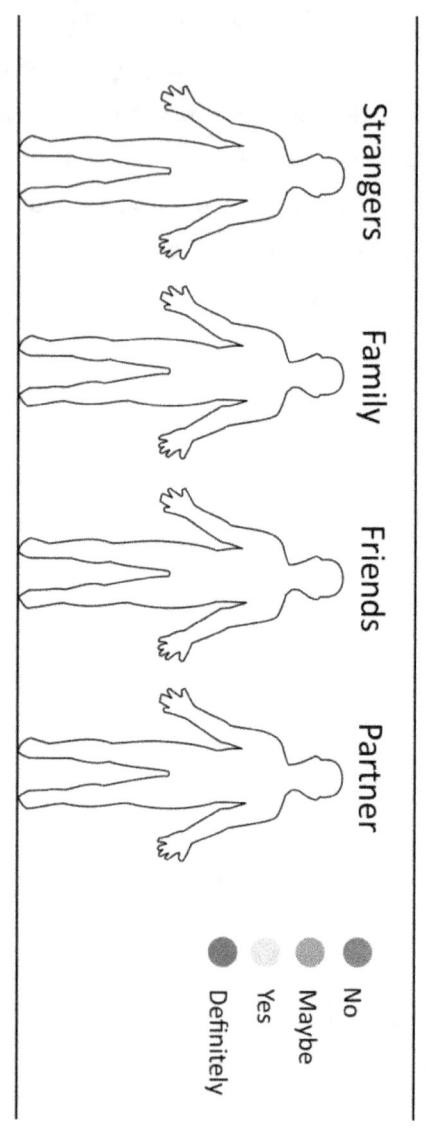

Family has more touch privileges, but not too much because it can get weird with family members that are much older than you or that you don't know well. Friends typically feel more comfortable because you are roughly the same age and the emotional connection is strong. Finally, most people would feel the most comfortable touch-wise when it comes to their partner.

To use this, you can print out the full version on the next page, and come up with your answer key. I've used red for 'no', orange for 'maybe', yellow for 'yes', and green for 'definitely'. Alternatively, you can also draw up your own map and use your own colours as well, as long as there's a key and it's the same one for your partner as well. Start with the first template. Stay true to yourself and colour it in honestly. Be as specific and non-specific as you want, but the more thought and detail you put into it, the more helpful it will be for yourself. Detail on the 'partner' template will also help them out to make sure you're comfortable. An example of detail would be, perhaps you don't really mind your partner touching your stomach area, but the sides? Hell yeah. You could shade the core yellow, and then use green on the sides. Get what I mean?

This is an example of a typical touch map you can get out of the template. Pretty neat, eh?

Doing stuff like this with your partner is just another form of communication, which is very beneficial.

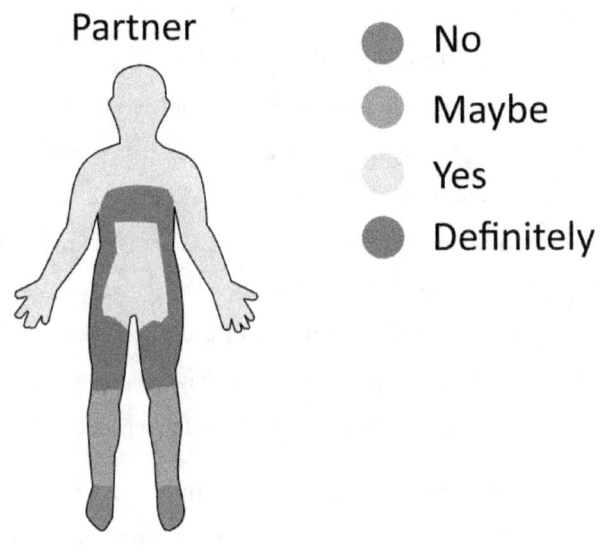

Love Addiction

Love can feel as terrible as it is wonderful. You can thank brain science for that. The hormones you feel when in love are the same ones you feel when you snort cocaine. Just putting it out there. As discussed previously, continued use of the reward pathways in our brain for these feel-good hormones can cause psychological damage.

Love addiction is very real. In general, addiction is defined as a compulsive and chronic pattern of behaviour for soothing uncomfortable feelings. A person who is addicted to love will find themselves constantly craving romantic affection from people to gain a sense of security and self-worth. It's really sad to say the least because just like drugs, addicts know that what they're doing isn't right, and that long-term craving can lead to negative consequences. But their dependency on the positive feelings of love is just too strong. People with love addiction find it hard to have healthy, committed relationships because they enter them for the **feelings**, not the person.

If you answer 'yes' to more than one of the questions below, you may be suffering from some degree of dependency on romantic love:

1. Do you feel that your life will only be happy if you find romantic love?

2. Are you pre-occupied with romance in entertainment (TV, books etc.)?

3. Do you date just for the sake of dating, or convince yourself into attraction?

4. Have you stayed in a bad relationship or stuck around an ex because you don't want to be alone?

5. Do periods of single-ness completely disrupt your life?

6. Do you find yourself constantly dating 'rebounds'?

7. Have you ever found yourself unable to move on from a failed relationship?

8. Do you find yourself pressuring your partner into making you feel loved?

Don't fret though. Like any other addiction, it can be treated. In order to do so, you need to break the addiction cycle.

1. **Admit that you are suffering love addiction.** Don't blame it on others and take full notice of your problematic pattern. Unless you're already in a relationship, don't engage in any sort of romantic interaction at all for 6 months. That's no dating websites, hook ups, texts or even introductions.

2. **If you're currently single, get some professional help before you look for love.** A self-evaluation will help to reduce the chance of your love addiction relapsing.

3. **Make a plan for you to follow daily.** What the plan should do is make you ask yourself what life would be like if you were to take responsibility of your own happiness, rather than relying on another person to love you. It should also make you reflect on your self-worth.

4. **Accept yourself and understand that you don't need a relationship to COMPLETE your life.** You're great just the way you are. Relationships are only supposed to ENHANCE it.

Withdrawal

At times, the treatment will make you feel sad and miserable. Substance users find themselves suffering mental and physical symptoms all the time when they start their path of rehabilitation. Withdrawal from love will hurt a lot, and you might find yourself suffering from self-doubt. But you need to stay strong. It'll be worth it when you finally lose the addiction!

Withdrawal can also occur for less-severe situations. You don't have to be an addict to suffer from it. That's because all of us will get used to the happy hormones you receive from love, to some degree. It hits especially hard if you don't see your partner frequently. In those periods of down-time, you'll find yourself unable to take your mind off them, and your general mood will go down until you can anticipate the next time you see them. Please note, that isn't a symptom of love addiction. It's pretty common for newer couples to do that (for more shenanigans about fresh couples, head to Living the Honeymoon). What makes it an addiction is when you find yourself unable to separate yourself from the thoughts and they haunt every moment of your waking (and not-waking) life.

Relationship dynamics (LGBT)

Society really likes to make roles. Like really. We're all familiar with the traditional male/female roles in a relationship, right? These dynamics have an influence on both physical and emotional aspects of a relationship. It's not necessarily a bad thing, it just sort of happens, like how gravity will always pull things downwards, you know?

The traditional view is that a man would court the girl like a gentleman, and when he gets the girl, he'll be a responsible man, in charge, who will do all the nitty gritty, because a lady shouldn't need to make big decisions and pay for bills. In sex, kind of the same thing. The guy always plays a more dominant role over the girl. And even then, all of this is becoming super outdated as time goes by. The new generations seem to have a knack of rejecting the traditional constructs of society.

That's because the system has limitations. It makes a whole lot of assumptions and to list a few:

1. There's a guy and girl involved.

2. It's a monogamous relationship.

3. The guy has more money than the girl.

4. The girl is fine with being passive.

5. The guy wants to top during sex.

Relationship dynamics are especially defined for LGBT couples because they themselves don't adhere to the more traditional roles. The binary of the traditional straight relationship is typically translated into personality, rather than gender, for non-straight relationships. It should be noted that top and bottom behaviour (both in sex and everyday life) aren't confined to gender, regardless of what society says. So when a clueless straight person asks who the 'man' in the relationship is, they're technically asking for who is the main 'driver' of the relationship. To make things even more complicated, top/bottom dynamics are also not directly translated sexually. Someone that is dominant in day-to-day life might want to be ordered around in bed. And yet again, your top/bottom status won't necessarily be related to whether you're a giver or a receiver ... and the factors go on and on.

The bottom line is, in this world of seven billion people, it's literally impossible for every single relationship to fit one model. Although it's not something that needs to be as heavily discussed as marriage, it's still something that is good to know.

Well, this has been a theory-heavy chapter. Brain stuff can be interesting if you like it, but if you don't it will all feel like waffle for you. Let's get back on track.

Part 7

Living the Honeymoon

The words 'I love you' taste like honey in your tongue and music to your ears. You're floating on cloud nine, and for once in your life you feel certain that this little thing you've got here is what was always meant to be. Well, whether that's true or not, you won't find out for a long while. And frankly ... who cares? Everything just feels so great right now.

The Butterflies

The beginnings of a relationship warrant intense euphoria and joy. It will feel like you're on top of the world when you go on your first date, then go on to calling each other cute pet names. Your mind will have a lot of fun imagining all the dates you can go on, all the sex you can have, and what the wedding will look like. The <u>honeymoon phase</u> gets a lot of bad rep because it represents the saccharine nature of romance. And most importantly, the honeymoon phase **does not last.** Just going to warn you now. But despite everyone using the honeymoon phase as a textbook example to prove why love is dead in the twenty-first century or whatever, you need to understand that it's inevitable to have that phase, especially if you're young or relatively new to dating. And that's ok.

Most experts agree that the honeymoon phase of a relationship refers to the first 2-3 years. That's when you're still getting used to the presence of your partner in your life. The whole idea of being drugged up on love hormones happen the most here. The brain will constantly seek out new things. That's why everyday seems super exciting with them. When time moves on and the amount of new things you can learn about someone starts to dwindle, you'll start getting used to them instead. Since infatuation is a precursor to love, there's also a chance that you two are feeling more infatuation than love in this stage, with the whole idealisation and obsession and whatnot.

How to tell you're in a honeymoon phase:

1. **You feel easily aroused by them.** Remember the 'lust' part of love. It'll be very intense during the honeymoon phase.

2. **You're constantly smiling when they're there.** Not that you'll stop smiling in a long-term relationship. I'm referring to the obnoxious laughing/smiling fresh couples do all the goddamn time.

3. **Their presence gives you butterflies.** You feel a lot of anticipation and nerves (in a good way) before seeing them.

4. **You two are constantly touching.** In the early points of relationships, couples will find themselves unable to keep their hands off each other. Affectionate contact produces a dose of oxytocin, after all.

5. **Your attention on them is hyper-focused.** If you two are at a party, you'll suddenly forget there are other people there.

6. **Everything they do is fine with you.** There's barely anything to disagree about. Or there are, but you find yourself doing/saying things you normally wouldn't like to do.

7. **The other parts of your life get a little neglected.** Your friends might be poking fun about having to constantly third wheel you (more on how to be a good third wheel is in chapter 10 - Earn Your Wings).

8. **You care a lot about how they think of you.** Yeah, you two are dating now ... but you still feel a pressure to maintain your appearance as if you're about to go on a blind date. You're not ready to fart in front of them yet.

9. **You find yourself full of energy.** You're constantly feeling exhilarated every time you're with them, even if the thing you're doing with them isn't that exciting.

10. **You're both a unit.** This might drive everyone insane, but you always say 'we' instead of just 'I'. Your partner has just become a large part of your identity.

I remember when I entered the honeymoon phase for the first time; I had to do a lot of research on it, along with the process of leaving the phase. It ruins the immersion to do that, of course. It's like spoiling an episode before you watch it. But while everyone is cynical about the whole notion, I've learnt to accept that you should be dumb and in love while you still can. But don't fear the next phase either. Every stage has its own beautiful portrayals of love.

This chapter is a starter kit for the new couple that is going through the honeymoon phase and just starting out on their relationship.

The Gist

It's not necessarily smooth sailing after getting into the relationship. Soon you'll find yourself needing to answer questions you've never even known were there before. Luckily for you, I've picked two of the biggest unspoken rules and explained them here so you can be more prepared.

The Internet

With the immersion of social media into our lives, of course it is going to affect dating too. One thing that really bewildered me in regards to that was the whole idea of being 'Facebook Official'. Like what? Posting about your relationship explicitly has become a milestone in twenty-first century dating. Not everyone cares about being 'Facebook Official', but it's good to talk about it with your partner. Either way, it won't hurt.

There are many reasons someone might want to opt out of being FO. They might dislike the 'exposure' social media gives and prefer to have a more private love life. They might not be social media savvy. Or they might be dating you in secret and don't want certain people to know. Especially because of the last reason, it's very important to ask your partner first before updating your relationship status on Facebook.

A lot of people comment that the integration of technology into dating has ruined it, though most of the problems come from finding a date online, rather than just posting after finding a relationship. As social media is visual, physical attraction is a bigger priority compared to regular dating in real life. People will feel a bit more pressured about maintaining a good image online. In general, social media has become a chore for some people, along with sorting out bills and washing the dishes.

Don't lie to yourself, maintaining your 'digital face' is absolutely tiring. So you can imagine it's even harder for couples. Just like the 'successful' people on Instagram who make you feel dumb and broke, the online presence of a couple doesn't reflect their real life. They probably fight, argue and have down time just like any other couple. The exhausting part of maintaining the online relationship is that it's exposed for thousands to see, so it can't be ugly. All the ugliness needs to be sorted out in private. This is the reason why many people, upon entering relationships, immediately declare they don't want to publicise their love life.

But hey, being FO can be a good thing too. Studies show that relational satisfaction can actually improve when people do couple photos for their profile display picture. Remember when I said earlier that people find it a struggle to share their love life to the online public? You can flip the problem of exposure into a benefit! Research shows that declaring the relationship on Facebook actually strengthened stability and security for some people. It's sort of like a digital wedding, and the witnesses are your friends and followers. And most people going to weddings are serious about their vows. Yet, if FO is a digital wedding, then the stakes would increase for leaving the relationship. You've just made it from a simple break-up to a digital divorce! Who's going to be your digital lawyer? Your digital counsellor? You know what I mean.

Personally, I once had a moderately-involved online relationship. When it ended, I had quite a lot of things to sort out, like removing statuses, deleting images, blocking my ex and changing my relationship status back to single. I guess the most amusing thing was the surprising efficiency we both showed while doing that. It was like we could just revert back to our original life, even though we were together for years. But for other people that are super, super involved online, as in full-on 'official couple pages' involved, it can be much more devastating.

So here are the two sides to dating and social media. It's up to your own preference and judgement to make a decision here.

The Parental Units

Here's another milestone that needs to be sorted out. This will definitely be a little after FO, but to be honest, your family will definitely see that you have updated your relationship status. In general, it's respectful to let you family and friends know that you're dating someone. It would be a bit weird for your son to disappear for 2 years and come back with a family of four. The concept of meeting parents is traditional and dates back to the 'man pulls out chairs and pays bills' era. Yes I know some younger folks reject every piece of traditional dating etiquette because it reminds them of heteronormativity and sexism, but I personally think meeting parents is a polite thing to do.

When would you NOT meet the parents? Well:

- ❖ Your/their parents are terrible people – that'll definitely give you both shit.

- ❖ Your/their parents are homophobic and you're in a gay relationship.

- ❖ Your/their parents are transphobic and one or both of you are trans.

- ❖ One or both you are not supposed to be dating.

- ❖ Your/their family background isn't ready for something like that.

Meeting their Parents

Alright, so your partner has decided it's time for their parents to meet you. Here's how to prepare to ensure that it will be a good experience for everyone involved:

First impressions – It's important for you to make a good first impression with their parents. As soon as they see you the assumptions will start, so be prepared. Make sure you dress appropriately and well. Physical appearance can represent a lot more than you think about a person. For an event like this, the safest dress code to opt for is smart casual. Unless explicitly told not to, it's good to bring a small gift of some sort. It doesn't have to be extravagant, just a little something for them to remember you. When greeting their parents, be friendly and polite. Do whatever they prompt you to do, as it can usually vary between a handshake to a hug and kiss on the cheek. Address your partner's parents politely. You don't usually use first names until you've made a few more visits or they ask you to.

During the event - Engage in conversation and be genuinely interested. For the time being, since you aren't close yet, refrain from swearing and politics. Praise your partner's parents appropriately, without overdoing it. In general, keep a calm demeanour. Although it's understandable that you'll be nervous, it won't make things better if you're constantly stuttering and looking down. Just take a few breaths and keep going. If you've been invited over, be a polite and pleasant houseguest by offering to clean up, refraining from touching random things, and following house rules.

When you leave - Let your partner's parents know you're leaving and tell them it was a pleasure to meet them. Go in for a hug or handshake depending on what they offer. For extra points, send them a small thank you note.

Meeting your Parents

There's no particular order for meeting your parents and their parents. But if you're the one bringing them home, here's what you do:

Make sure you're ready - Meeting parents is a milestone that requires both you and your partner to feel emotionally ready in this point of the relationship. The best time to do it is between the first 6 to 12 months. That's when the relationship is still fresh but it's solidified enough for you to determine if it's serious or not. Too early and your partner will feel a little overwhelmed by the quick advancement. Too late, your parents will feel disrespected that you're holding back on such an important aspect of your life.

Prepping your parents – tell them about your relationship if you haven't already. If they don't give you a positive reaction, don't proceed. If they do, arrange a time for meeting. The usual event for this is dinner at home, but any other location for casual drinks and food is fine too. Most parents, being from a more traditional era, would like it to be at home where they feel the most comfortable. Give your parents some background information about the relationship so they can talk to your partner. Maybe tell them about the newest project you two are working on, or a show that you both discovered and enjoy. Next, do the opposite and tell your parents topics to not talk about. These topics may be ones that will warrant a negative reaction or are just way too heavy to be discussed at the moment. You need to make sure both parties are comfortable when talking over a meal. The last thing to do is to remind your parents of dietary requirements that your partner has so they can prepare food and refreshments accordingly if the event is hosted at your house.

Prepping your partner – If you're bringing your partner home, you'll be fully comfortable being surrounded with people you talk to all the time, but remember that your partner may feel nervous. Before the meeting, let them know that it'll be okay and you'll be there to make sure things go smoothly. Update your partner on any drama happening in your family. You don't need to give them a 200-page dossier, but they should understand roughly what everyone is up to at the moment, what job they do, what goals they have etc. This sort of serves the same purpose as telling your parents topics to avoid. This way, your partner can tread carefully with conversation and not get sucked into any drama so quickly. If your partner is planning on giving your parents a gift, walk them through that and help them out. Receiving a good gift will definitely increase your parent's approval of your partner. Identify the common grounds that your partner may share with your parents. This can be used to their advantage for approval and conversation. Finally, if the event is at your house, make your partner is a good houseguest by telling them house rules.

During the dinner – Don't be tense or it'll rub off on your parents and partner. Get your head out of the lasagne and be extra vigilante about the interactions happening. If the conversation feels like it's going to turn sour, change the topic. If there's an awkward silence building up, be the one to initiate a conversation that will include both parties. Offer your partner food and drinks, especially if the event is in your house. They won't be 100% sure where everything is in the kitchen and they'll most likely be too shy to ask. Stay close to them for the whole night, even if you're tempted to go around and talk to family members. When you're this early on in a relationship, it's highly likely the only person they'll be comfortable enough to interact with will be you. Although it would be natural for your date to be the centre of interest, don't let your family members crowd them too much as they may feel overwhelmed with all the interaction. If they seem to be comfortable in the environment, let them make their own way.

Seeing their children develop a romantic relationship is big for parents. To them, you were a child only yesterday. The thought that their baby will be giving their affection to someone else apart from themselves is going to produce a lot of mixed emotions. Some parents will just see it as part of life and congratulate you for moving on to a new chapter. Other parents may feel bitter about you being in a relationship as it represents losing control over you. Regardless of what your parents are like, always stay true to yourself. Try your best to maintain the best diplomatic ties between your family and partner. If things go well, eventually your partner will join your family circle anyway.

The Ingredients to a Healthy Relationship

You and your partner are baking a cake right now as we speak. Your relationship that you're currently developing is a cake with its very own ingredients. Like any baking recipe, each ingredient isn't very interesting alone, but none of them can be missing from the cake or else it'll taste weird.

Relationship Cake (serves 2)

Utensils

- ❖ You
- ❖ Your partner
- ❖ Willingness to put effort into the relationship

Cake base

- ❖ Honesty
- ❖ Communication
- ❖ Compromise
- ❖ Respect
- ❖ Support
- ❖ Patience
- ❖ Devotion

Icing

- ❖ Laughter
- ❖ Sex
- ❖ Affection
- ❖ Intellectual Compatibility

Method

1. Love requires you to be **honest**. Even if the truth isn't ideal, it is still crucial that it is heard. Built-up dishonesty will get you in hot water later on.

2. **Communication** is always vital. If you and your partner never argue or fight over anything, that might not be ideal. Yes, constant fighting is also a sign of a bad relationship but fighting allows growth. A good fight will always lead to improvements. Poor communication results in built up resentment. I'll talk more about this in part 8.

3. No matter how in-tune you and your partner are, there will be times where you need to **compromise**. Stubbornness will harm your relationship when disputes happen. Learning to effortlessly compromise for small things, like where to eat, will make you two more prepared when needing to compromise for bigger things in the future, like which city to move to or what house to buy.

4. **Respect** is a no-brainer. If you two aren't respecting each other as individuals with feelings, then what's the point of being in a relationship? Embrace the things that make your partner unique.

5. You need to be each other's **support** network. Co-dependency isn't good of course, but the amount of emotional intimacy that you'll share with your partner means they'll likely be comfortable being vulnerable in front of you. Don't take advantage of that. Instead, stand with them when they need it.

6. Relationships won't be perfect first try. There will be times where things are just frustrating for you and your partner. Be **patient** and things will improve.

7. It can be hard to be fully **devoted**, especially when the honeymoon phase wears off, but it's vital that you mustn't give up.

8. Relationships aren't supposed to be super serious. Sometimes people whose honeymoon periods have long faded forget that love can be fun. **Laughter** can be rejuvenating for you and your partner and reduce tension.

9. Now, not everyone likes **sex,** and that's okay. However, the key ingredient here is physical intimacy. Physical intimacy makes a person feel wanted, cared for and loved. And those are the exact things you'd look for when in a relationship, right?

10. Similarly, **affection** in a relationship adds to the sweeter, more pleasant side of the relationship. Physical attraction is shunned by many progressive people, but it's as important as emotional attraction when it comes to making relationships last.

11. It's pretty hard to be in a relationship with someone who doesn't share any common views with you, right? Not a lot of people consider **intellectual compatibility** to be important, but it is. While healthy fights will allow you to grow, intellectual incompatibility is just going to make you resent them.

The preparation time will be around 2 years in total. Once the cake base is prepared (and it's a nice and solid foundation), you can add the icing.

Remember, the cake will require both you and your partner to work together. No single ingredient can be left out. If you find that your partner's really not putting effort into the cake, tell them to leave the kitchen and find someone else that will try harder. Seriously, it's just going to be a waste of time and effort on your part if they don't try.

First Things First

With a first relationship, there's definitely going to be a whole load of other firsts as well. If I went through all of them, this book will never end, so I'll only run you through some important things. As for first sexual encounters, you'll have to go get another source. Previously, the section on meeting parents already encompasses a 'first', which is seeing family.

First Valentine's Day - Ah yes, Valentine's Day is always met with mixed reactions. A lot of people hate it because it feels 'commercial' or something like that. Valentine's Day first began as just a Christian holiday for the martyr Saint Valentine. Through the ages, corporations hopped on board to make the holiday's romantic theme really come up. Some people feel like it's just a random excuse in the year to buy shit and reinforce the over-saturation of romance that is present in society. Alternatively, it makes people that are single or aren't interested in romance (aromantic folk) feel terrible. But hey, Valentine's Day can be awesome too.

Because lots of people care about it, you'll feel that your feelings about your partner may generally increase that day. It's just part of the atmosphere. Nonetheless, a lot of couples stress out about celebrating their first V Day. The most important thing to do is, of course, to discuss it. Find out if they even acknowledge V Day in the first place. If you both decide that you want to do it, next you have to think of how to celebrate. Since you're still relatively early into the relationship, it's okay to start simple and cliché. Invite your partner to dinner. Give them a gift. Go see a movie. Revel in the cheesiness of the holiday. As the relationship progresses, you might reach a point where neither of you feel the need to celebrate Valentine's Day anymore.

First anniversary - Just like Valentine's Day, not everyone likes to celebrate dating anniversaries. That's because they don't pack the same significance as a wedding anniversary. But for now, if you and your partner would still like to celebrate it, here's how. Many people on anniversaries like to sum up all the fun things they've done in the past years of their relationship. Since your first anniversary marks one year, there might not be a lot for you to work on. Instead, you can focus more about all the positive things they've made you feel since becoming part of your life.

People usually go on the same type of dates for anniversaries as any other regular event. So it's fine to just take your partner out to dinner or go for a walk at the beach. To make the date more special (well, it *is* an anniversary after all), people sometimes give flowers and personalised gifts that they wouldn't give for just regular dates. Unlike V Day, anniversaries probably won't tackier as the time goes. This will be especially vital as the relationship progresses and the fluffy, romantic feelings become scarce. More on that will come during Part 8, The Long Haul of Death.

The great thing about firsts in a relationship is that each thing will preview how they'll be in the long term. Here's a couple of things that you should consider (you don't have to, of course, but this will help) doing with your partner before hitting the 1-year mark.

1. **Cooking together** – It's a great way to connect. It's also a way to see how you and your partner will tackle tasks together. Maybe one of you has more cooking expertise and will boss the other person around. Maybe you both have absolutely no clue what to do but you're willing to work together and learn something new.

2. **Having a weekend trip** – I mean, isn't it nice to have a short and sweet getaway? This could just be a little road trip or weekend city break or something like that. It can give you an idea of what they're like domestically and also it's a great way to bond. Maybe you'll learn that they snore, or that they don't hang up their towels.

3. **Going abroad** – If you can afford it, go on a holiday with them that requires a bit more travel. This one doesn't necessarily have to be just the two of you; family and friends can be included too. It'll create some nice memories. And just like the above suggestion, going abroad reveals their attitude on travelling, other cultures and their off-duty personality.

4. **Meeting parents** – As described previously.

5. **Run errands** – Unless you're living with your partner, you're probably not going to be there with them to do most mundane things like going to the grocery store or returning a book to the library. However, if you have the opportunity to run an errand with them, it can be quite interesting and

beneficial to the relationship. That's because it helps you get used to their presence (not every day of your relationship is going to be a fun-filled date), and see how they deal with everyday life.

Relationship Check-up

You've just arrived at your first relationship check up! Just like a car, you need to talk to your partner regularly about the relationship to smooth out any problems before they become unsolvable and cause problems. Regarding this, I'll provide you with a troubleshooting guide in part 8. The recommended interval between check-ups is the first six months, then the first year, then after that, just check up every anniversary. You should still be doing smaller check-ups throughout the year though.

Maintenance Checklist

To use the checklist, find a convenient time for you and your partner to talk. Please don't actually hold a clipboard and tick things off FBI-style. Just have an easy-going conversation, or it will feel too tense.

Then, you can just go through each question with them. If they're intuitive enough, they'll know what you're doing and ask you back. If not, just explain to them that you'd like to check in with them. Your partner will most likely get the idea and ask you some questions afterwards to check in with you.

- ☐ How are you feeling about our pace? Are we going too fast? (we covered this in Part 5)
- ☐ Are there any particular issues that need to be addressed?
- ☐ What would be the next step for you? When do you want to achieve this?

- ☐ Are you still emotionally okay having a relationship right now?

- ☐ Is there something you want us to start doing?

- ☐ Is there something you want us to stop doing?

Many couples who have broken up think that their relationship has spontaneously fallen apart. In reality, that doesn't just happen. There would have been many warning signs of cracks in the relationship that both people are ignoring or misunderstanding. When these issues are noticed, some people choose to ignore them or distract themselves, just as someone would turn up their radio to stop hearing the weirding clanking noise in their car. Just because you can't see something doesn't mean it's not there. It's not fun to admit a problem and try to fix it, but it's even worse to see a relationship fall apart. Want to know more about what happens when a relationship does fail?

Love Blindness

When I was young, I developed a bad habit. I'd always blink my eyes in an erratic way. Thinking it was just some tic, my parents would pinch my eyelids until I was physically in pain. I mean, even if it was a tic, it wouldn't have been an effective treatment. Eventually, my parents took me to an optometrist to see what was wrong. I was diagnosed with myopia (short-sightedness) at 9, which wasn't very surprising as I come from a family with a history of poor eye health. Yet, I never really knew it was there until I had it checked out. Not long after that, I got my first prescription glasses. I can still remember staring at a blurry advert poster at the end of the optometrist's office. Carefully, I put my glasses on and as soon as I had, it was as though my whole life changed. Right in front of me, everything shifted into a level of clarity that I had never seen before.

Just like eye problems, love can cloud a person's judgement. We call that 'love blindness'. This happens especially during the earlier periods of relationships when you're still infatuated with your partner. For a quick refresher, here's what infatuations are: a superficial feeling of attraction.

When you're infatuated with someone, you're attracted to the idea of them, rather than the actual individual. Mixed with the chemical high that romance gives, infatuations provide you lots of fun and thoroughly convince you that you're dating the ultimate embodiment of perfection. There's nothing wrong with loving your partner as who they are and seeing them as an amazing individual, but infatuations are just an artificial sweetener that can have negative effects such as jealousy, obsession and disappointment.

You might think that this only happens when you're crushing on someone or before you've had your second date, but 'love blindness' can still be present when the traditional time period of infatuation is over. You can observe it even in couples that have become stabilised. It's pretty irritating as an observer when you see your friend or family member tirelessly defend the subpar and even toxic behaviours of their partner. Or when they come to you completely shattered after a disagreement even though you had warned them about the issue ages ago.

To make sure that you're not suffering from love blindness, I've got a free eye check for you. If you agree to some of these things, you may have love blindness.

1. **You're at an unhealthy distance from family and friends.** New couples always end up being too exclusive by accident in their early days. But if you're finding yourself dedicating disproportionately large amount of time in the relationship and not anybody else, we've got a problem here. It's risky to have that distance, as it creates a reliance on your partner to be your sole support system and hurts your trust with family and friends. Since they're not in your relationship, they can see the situation from a better angle and give you helpful advice. To lose them will be very risky.

2. **You find yourself changing to accommodate the relationship.** You may be so obsessed with keeping the relationship happy that you find yourself starting to do things you normally wouldn't. Yes, personal growth can happen in relationships and the both of you can come out of it as better people. But cutting your hair or not eating your favourite food because of your partner? That's love blindness.

3. **You're making major decisions too early.** Infatuations convince us that our relationship is perfect. This means you'll most likely skip out on the nervous water-testing phase in the beginning and jump right into it. You need to constantly check your pacing with, not only your partner, but yourself. Major decisions like moving in, merging bank accounts etc. all increase the damage you'll take if the relationship fails. If you haven't even gone past the honeymoon phase yet and you're already doing those things, you need to pause and think.

4. **You're ignoring red flags.** Sure everyone has flaws, but if you're love blind, you'll find yourself immediately forgiving your partner without analysing the situation. Not only that, you wouldn't encourage their redemption or change. For couples to grow, mistakes need to be fully acknowledged. If your partner promises to change, you need to make sure they actually GO ALONG WITH IT. What relationship red flags actually are will be discussed later on.

5. **You excuse their bad behaviour.** You'll develop a perpetual bias towards your partner over almost everything. As infatuations make you see someone in the best light, you'll let slide their bad behaviours that you otherwise wouldn't tolerate in others. Too many times have I have seen girls that are generally progressive date a guy and let their problematic behaviour slide. Worse yet, I've seen girls turn more and more racist or homophobic for their partners.

If you ever find yourself love blind, don't panic. Even though your relationship may be established by now, it's not too late to fix it. If your partner doesn't believe in the above problems, then you should consider leaving.

50 Relationship Red Flags

Let's quickly get one thing clear, <u>red flags</u> refer to 'warning signs' that may indicate your relationship has a risk of causing you harm. In other words, they signpost that your partner may be toxic and it's not beneficial for you to stay in a relationship with them. Uncovering these red flags isn't a pleasant experience. Not only will they completely shatter the rose-coloured lenses you've always seen them in, but it may cause you to feel bad about yourself for getting into the relationship in the first place. But the earlier you can detect them and leave, the better. Toxic relationships can deal life-long damage. It will mess you up to the point you'll feel like it's your OWN fault. But always remember that it is NEVER your fault. To learn more about toxic relationships, The Silent Hand in part 8 is the place to go.

The list of red flags is expansive. These are just 50 of them, and each varies in subtlety. No matter how big or small, a red flag is still a red flag for a much bigger issue.

1. They don't apologise for bad behaviour.
2. They don't see a common denominator with past relationships.
3. They use ultimatums to get their way.
4. Their reply rate online is poor (given that they have reliable access to their phone).
5. They have problematic friends.

6. They constantly bring up things you've done wrong in the past.

7. They get upset when you hang out with friends and family.

8. They constantly talk about past relationships.

9. They keep the relationship completely hidden. (Away from certain toxic people is understandable but ... from the entire world? That's not a real relationship at all).

10. They don't seem to get along with many people.

11. They never tell the full truth and leave out parts that make you upset.

12. They are emotionally unstable over little things.

13. Their family aren't abusive or anything, but your partner treats them like shit.

14. They make rules for you.

15. They refuse to get close to your (not abusive) family.

16. You find yourself always apologising.

17. They're overly defensive about their personal devices.

18. They don't provide you emotional support when you need it.

19. They're rude to service workers.

20. They get angry and defensive when discussing their mistakes.

21. They can make a negative comment about literally anything.

22. They cheated on someone to be with you.
23. They're surrounded by people that consider them romantically.
24. They don't show interest in what's important to you.
25. They don't compliment you or say thanks.
26. They continuously preach their independence.
27. They have a history of substance/alcohol abuse.
28. They're extremely moody (for no reason at all).
29. They enforce double standards on you.
30. They're still looking at their ex's social media.
31. They have unrealistic expectations on the relationship.
32. They don't care about things that don't directly affect them.
33. They are toxic and aggressive when drunk (a person's drunk self is their uninhibited self after all).
34. They barely put any work into making things right after a fight.
35. They actually enjoy the drama of fighting and the excitement it brings.
36. They don't respect themselves, you or the relationship.
37. Their relationship history is problematic.

38. They project their problematic traits onto you, but maybe don't realise.

39. Their family (given not abusive) doesn't think you two will last.

40. They put you down a lot.

41. They're constantly deleting texts and erasing online records of communication.

42. They change completely after the honeymoon phase.

43. They say, 'I always get what I want'.

44. They have no work ethic.

45. They lie about even mundane things.

46. They are nervous about texts and calls they receive.

47. They grew up in an unstable background.

48. They are very loud when angry.

49. They have an excuse for everything.

50. They're constantly testing your boundaries.

We're now starting to hit the not-so-fun parts of a relationship. The real stuff. Sit tight for the remaining chapters. They won't be very nice topics, but they are important.

Part 8

The Long Haul of Death

First it was the lack of reply, and then it was a period of complete silence. They're always busy. You're always busy. Life is just busy. It's completely understandable though, right? Maybe something's up with them, and as much as you want to know what's up so you can make things better, there's something in your heart that is telling you not to.

The next thing to get hit was the time you spent with them. It just wasn't happening as much as it used to. Even when you two did get together, the feelings just weren't the same anymore. Where's the kissing that would leave you dizzy with delight? Where's the complete deconstruction of time when you gazed into their eyes? Only months ago, time would freeze when you two were together. Now, you just wish for time to go faster. It's then that you learn that your whole world has changed and, if you don't change along with it, you'll go down.

When the Well Runs Dry

The honeymoon phase, like any other thing in the world, will eventually fade. What comes next is commonly known as the <u>long haul</u>. Whether your relationship is soon reaching this point, has already reached this point or you're just reading this chapter for the future, I'm here to give you a sincere warning of what is to come. Listen carefully:

When the long haul comes, the feelings of the relationship will change. Getting to know your partner will also mean throwing away the rose-coloured lenses and seeing all their ugliness and scars. The level of commitment and intimacy needed for a long-term relationship will be more apparent. Many people will be scared and pull back. Or they will fight over insecurities that were hidden prior to the long haul. When this happens, the couple will lose their compatibility and the romantic feelings of the relationship.

Although that sounds ominous, it doesn't mean that your relationship is a lost cause. It just means that it won't be easy. And it really isn't. Around 70% of couples break-up at the 2-year mark. Yep, you've read it right. 70%. And since you're now knowledgeable about relationship pacing, do you know what also happens at the 2-year mark? The end of the honeymoon phase!

Although this chapter is going to get down to the nitty-gritty of the ugliness of love, I'm not just going to leave you all defeated and depressed. I'll also be covering the ways to save your relationship from the long haul of death, and how to strengthen it for the future. Although the shift breaks up a lot of people, statistics also show that when you get beyond that, the break-up rate starts to decrease. There definitely is a stabilisation that can be achieved. If that weren't the case, you wouldn't see so many old couples around. But they do exist, and that's because they've cracked the code.

Love is Not Lost, Just Evolved

Around the early years of the long haul, many couples complain about a loss of romantic love. In their honeymoon period, they'd always go on exciting dates and have a great sex life. Now, they no longer squash up together on movie nights; they sit on opposite sides of the room. They now only have sex once a month, when they aren't busy. They don't kiss as often, and when they do, they're quick 'goodbye' kisses. So what happened? Did the relationship's love die with the honeymoon phase?

The answer is no. If love just died with the honeymoon phase, we wouldn't see any long-term couples around at all. The love is still there, it's just different. I could spend a long time explaining this but the bigger picture is that the love has turned from thrill to safety. Say it after me. Thrill to safety.

A lot of people say that the feeling of love makes you feel safe but vulnerable at the same time. If we were to use this as our measurement, it would be correct to say that as time goes on, the 'safe' part becomes more prominent than the 'vulnerable' part. It's just something that we have to get used to. Unfortunately, a lot of young couples really don't know that this is supposed to happen. They write it off as the death of their 'spark'. Come on, let's be realistic here. You can't expect the relationship to be rainbows and butterflies forever. Perhaps it's the 'right now' attitude of the new generation that makes their relationships more susceptible to dying in the long haul. A relationship's honeymoon phase gives a lot of 'right now's. Make out session? Sure, let's do it. Can we go on a date tomorrow? Tomorrow night, got it. Wanna have sex right now? I sure do. A long-term relationship requires people who can comprehend delayed gratification. In fact, the entire relationship is pretty much delayed gratification. You plant the seeds of love now and in the future you get a strong bond for life.

Unfortunate Downfalls of the High-School Sweethearts

What's the most popular face of young love in the media? They are the hand-holding, jersey-wearing <u>high-school sweethearts.</u> High school is the time where a person will most likely experience sex and romance for the first time. Despite parents telling you that they don't want you to date in high school, let me tell you something: they dated in high school too. High school relationships start as easily as they end. If you're observant and are friends with people that are open to dating, you'll notice that. Of course, there'll always be exceptions, but most of the time, they are quite fickle.

Why? Well let's take a look here. Remember my entire section on teenage brains? Teenagers are still developing physically and mentally. They've only just started to understand the world of romance and sex. Mix that with peer pressure and media oversaturation of romance, you've got yourself a bunch of horny, desperate teenagers. Of course, not everyone's like that, but the fact that someone in high school already has an idea of what true love is like tells you that they're affected. Many teenagers are hooking up and getting into relationships just for the sake of it. It's become an achievement, a box to tick off, rather than an actual commitment. I don't mean to be rude but, choosing someone in your school to cuff is pretty much the equivalent of choosing the best apple from one single tree, when you're standing in an entire orchard. Like ... yes, it's the best from *that* tree but look around you! There are a hundred other trees you can look at!!!

Okay, so our hypothetical teenage girl here has managed to choose one guy in the high school who is relatively suitable. If you're a girl, generally you'll find it's easier to hook up than to cuff a guy. Why? Because male mental maturity is still catching up to a female's in high school. It's going to be many, and I mean MANY, years before they finally fully get there at 43 – that's 11 years after a woman does. That's probably an exaggeration, but that was the number that a study commissioned by Nickelodeon UK in 2013 calculated. But either way, it is a biological fact that guys arrive late to the puberty party. It takes more maturity for successful relationships than hook ups.

This hypothetical teenager's relationship is going pretty well with the dude. Their status has spread around schools. They attend house parties together and make out on the couch. They take photos and put them on the Internet with fire and heart emojis. Both the guy's friends and the girl's friends are fine with their pal's choice of partner. Occasionally, the couple have some conversations, but most of them are post-coitus and don't concern the future.

Graduation comes. They celebrate their anniversary, and promise each other they will Face-Time each other every day now they're going to different universities. And then they break-up 3 months later. So why do high-school sweethearts die as soon as they leave school? Well here are some things that might happen to them individually as they settle into university life:

1. **You'll feel dragged down.** High school will become an old chapter in your life when you graduate. Most of the time, you have to wipe your slate clean to continue the next segment. A high-school sweetheart is a relic of that old chapter, which was full of school uniforms, school bells and bonding by proximity. If you're someone that really wants a new life after a rather unpleasant experience in high school, your partner is not going to help.

2. **You'll realise your world is bigger now.** High school is a fish tank, and university is an aquarium – not quite as big as the ocean, but definitely much more unrestricted and diverse than previously. University is a melting pot after all. You might meet people that were from a different school or home town who interest you much more than your current partner.

3. **You'll let the distance get you.** If you and your partner went to the same high school and aren't joining the same course at the same university, you'll suffer from a sudden increase in distance. While some people can handle it, it will definitely be difficult. Mixed in with the paranoia of cheating, 'finding someone better' and whatnot, many couples fall apart just because of the fact they're not seeing each other five days a week anymore.

4. **You'll be different from your high-school self.** Every big 'shift' in life changes into your character drastically. Graduating high school is one of them. You and your partner will gain a lot of new experiences at university and that might negatively affect your compatibility with them.

The most important thing if you choose to try to keep your high school relationship going is to not fake it. If during your university years you find yourself feeling romantic about someone else or your feelings about your current partner are starting to fade, you need to own up to it. I understand that it's hard, but you and your partner need to talk about this. Here's a pledge you two can both take (not seriously like a ritual though, that's creepy):

I pledge that while I'll maintain my commitment in this relationship, if my heart was to change due to university life and I am no longer attracted to you, I'll be honest about these feelings and communicate them to you.

This will be a very difficult pledge, understandably. After all, everyone enters a relationship hoping it will be their last. But hey, love isn't easy. And it's especially not easy when you're transitioning from high-school sweethearts into something more.

Right now, you might be thinking, 'wow what the hell, I picked up this book to learn how to be in a relationship and now you're just telling me that I'm going to fail?' Before you throw this book out of your window, I'm just going to say that it is POSSIBLE to survive, okay? It all sounds pretty gloomy right now, but hey, in very rare occasions, high-school sweethearts can work out.

And now, for the part you're all waiting for.

Eight things to do to make it work:

1. **You've both made the pledge and are prepared for the worst.** Constantly worrying about breaking up isn't good either, but as long as you two are conscious that it might happen, this means that you and your partner have excellent communication and understanding of your relationship.

2. **Make sure you're on the same page.** Since people in high school are still undergoing development, maturity can have a bit of a free pass. Girls don't mind their boyfriends smoking weed and making pterodactyl noises because 'boys will be boys'. Couples who have a clear dynamic where one person is very responsible and the other acts like a child is cute and 'quirky' in high school, but when the future hits, these types of relationships will quickly break down. That's because the mature one will get even more mature at university, while the immature one will most likely find themselves unable to keep up. When a relationship goes into the long haul, there's going to be a lot of things that need sorting out that aren't necessarily fun.

3. **Sort out all the things you're worried about.** The half worry/half high period of your relationship should be over. If by the time you're at university you are still head-over-heels for your partner and they make you worried about how the relationship would work and how you would keep them, then you're in a risky situation. That essentially means that you're entering university in a relationship in the honeymoon phase. Even people in stable relationships can fail at this point, so you can pretty much guarantee a honeymoon relationship is an immediate fail.

4. **Put serious effort into seeing each other.** There's a pretty big chance you won't be seeing them much now. You might think without a set schedule of school it'll be easier to see them. You'll be surprised at how much effort you actually have to put in now. It's nice to have some distance because it allows personal growth, but unless you're LDR, not seeing the other person physically will harm the relationship. To make it easier, both of you could join an outside-of-school activity that will guarantee at least fixed meetings. On top of that, don't be lazy and actually plan dates.

5. **Be realistic.** If your relationship was a sword, you need to be its maker. You need to know it thoroughly, including all its strengths and its weak points. Every relationship has its weak points that can cause you to break apart and there's not much you can do about it. Pulling your head out of the clouds and understanding that will greatly benefit not only your relationship, but your own mental health. It'll be easier to do this when you're past the honeymoon period.

6. **Choose your battles.** If you haven't had a serious fight with your partner yet and think you're both agreeable, then oh boy, wait till university - you'll have yours. There'll be times when things just frustrate both of you. It's too mentally exhausting to constantly deal with all of them. You need to learn to be mature and let some more insignificant things go. What's more important, your ego or your relationship? Later on in this chapter, we'll talk more about fighting with your partner in a beneficial way.

7. **Get out of social media's artificiality.** Putting cute couple edits and couple Instagram accounts (yes, they exist) are what teenagers do. You two will be adults soon. Remember, you've read a whole section on social media (if you haven't, it's in Part 7), and you know that stuff doesn't necessarily help. You can still do FO and share photos, but the more online PDA, the more exhausting it is to maintain what the public sees.

8. **Have the same goals.** We often assume that our partner has the same motives as us when we date. Otherwise, how would we mix together so well? But sometimes, we can all have ulterior motives or just have wildly different ideas of how a relationship works. When you head to university, you need to be very sure that you both want the same thing. Do you both want an open relationship where the other can still date? Are you two just looking for sex? Do you both see a need to see each other frequently?

My high school relationship didn't make it. And because I can't rewind my life, I can't make things right again and tell you what it feels like to have a high school relationship that lasts after graduation. This may decrease my credibility here, but I believe in honesty for my dear readers. Despite the loss of my own high school relationship, I don't doubt the possibility of it working for others. We're all human – I too experienced confusion and made mistakes during adolescence, but I'm optimistic for others that prevailed.

So you know what? Have a go. If you are serious about making your relationship last while at university, I seriously wish you all the best. I hope that you'll have the endurance, the faith, the commitment and the love to let it happen. If you find yourself breaking off, I'd also like to say that it's okay. It doesn't mean that you're not loveable or anything, though it might take a lot of emotional strength to heal from the disappointment. There'll be more on break-ups further down this chapter.

Forever means Forever

I just want to let you know I'm a Buddhist. Just a regular devotee who doesn't meditate every day or practice vegetarianism. I know you probably think I'm being off-topic here but bear with me. One important principle of Buddhism is that of 'impermanence'. That means that every single thing in the universe, as in, every single thing, will change. You see, not everyone's Buddhist, so most people don't give half a damn about what impermanence is. Because of that, the concept of 'eternity' plagues all our work poetically and theoretically. Look at romantic love. The theme of 'forever' sneaks in here and there all the time. And notice that none of the 'forevers' are certain. Weddings are supposed to be a bond for life, yet more than 50% of couples divorce. People who say, 'I love you', which is supposed to be a statement that represents an infinite stretch of time, can probably cheat or fall out of love if they want to. The love locks that couples put on bridges, well, they're going to degrade and come apart eventually.

High-school sweetheart or not, relationships need work to be put into them, or they just won't last. Despite society persistently marketing romantic love as fun, it's not all rainbows and unicorns. The 'work' that you put into it will sometimes feel like a drag. You'll feel frustrated. But the reward you earn is something that gives life such a rich purpose.

No one starts off completely prepared to have a healthy, long-term relationship. That's why heartbreak happens. It's good to know that good relationship skills can be learnt, because that means we all have a chance.

A Summary of What You'll Need

Remember when we listed all the ingredients needed for a healthy relationship cake? Well, here's a quick summary of principles that will be especially useful in baking a relationship cake that will survive:

1. **Knowing the things that brought you two together** – believe it or not, after a while together, couples lose their spark and desire. They've gotten too used to each other and caught up with other parts of their lives. Maintaining the very things that made you fall in love with your partner, and the things that remind you of the early, sweet days of dating will avoid the built-up resentment and lack of affection that breaks people up.

2. **Honesty and trust** – Honesty and trust make up the backbone of a relationship's emotional side, which is slightly more important than the physical side. After all, a romantic relationship will be one of the most vulnerable types of relationships. As I've said time and time again, honesty is absolutely golden. Lying now may make the situation good, but continual lying is something that will stack up. Romantic relationships are supposed to be intimate, so what's the point if you can't even open up and be honest with them?

3. **Resilience** – The ability to stick around even if things are tough. It's easy to walk away, but that doesn't mean it's the right thing to do (of course, sometimes you do have to walk away, read on for The Silent Hand). Even love – one of the best aspects of life – has ugliness that needs to be addressed. To have a heart that won't give up at the slightest inconvenience not only means you're an emotionally sound person, but it also demonstrates that you genuinely love your partner enough to sort problems out with them, rather than just quitting.

4. **Fun** – On the flip side, of course, you need to learn to have fun. Being able to laugh off mistakes brings down the overall tension in a relationship. This is especially important if your relationship is already tense due to external circumstances. Laughing increases your oxytocin levels which then improves the bonding between you and your partner. Having fun also links back to point one and brings back the happy feelings felt in the honeymoon phase.

So, those are the main things you'll need to make sure your relationship is on the right track to survive the long haul. Sure, those ingredients decrease the likelihood of a relationship encountering problems, but what if you do run into problems? Well, when that happens, there's also ways to deal with them.

Quick Relationship Troubleshooting

Before you read this, just remember that this is only a quick guide for general issues. It's impossible to solve relationship problems with just a book. Every issue is personal and unique to the situation and people involved. In order to solve relationship problems, the best way is to sit down with your partner and properly communicate to each other about it. Come up with a solution that both of you are willing to do and doesn't disadvantage anyone.

1. **Infidelity** – The reality is that 50% of people have had affairs. Society manages to normalise infidelity in a way that it becomes a punchline, but what society has also normalised is toxic monogamy. What the hell is that, you may ask. Toxic monogamy culture is the reinforced idea that romantic relationships between two people are very exclusive, when the reality is that humans are not monogamous by nature. Yes, you heard right. Notice how society really talks about the power of 'two'? Even the term 'other half' is used when referring to one's partner. Because of that, when a person actually is polygamous in nature, they start to struggle under the stress of staying monogamous. Despite all of that, cheaters still deserve no sympathy as an affair is something secretive. And as you know, that's a lack of respect to your partner. If your relationship is suffering from this problem, try to sit down and talk about it, instead of resolving to violence.

Find out the cause of the infidelity. No one ever cheats without a reason. If it is you who has cheated, assess yourself. Is it because you feel confined in a monogamous relationship? Have you lost physical attraction for your partner? If your partner was the cheater, make sure they are honest with their reason. Keep in mind that intoxication is not a valid justification. All intoxication does is make you more likely to act on the reason that's already in your mind. After the underlying issue is exposed, aim to resolve it. Do this while keeping in mind that the cheater will still need to apologise as cheating is a lack of trust and respect. The solution might be to have an open relationship or go to counselling. Either way, a solution can only be achieved if both parties can address it maturely.

2. **Sexual incompatibility** - If both people in a relationship are allosexual (that is, not asexual), then sex and physical intimacy can be a pretty big deal. Therefore, sexual problems can have a big negative impact on a relationship. One common issue is that of libido. What happens if you're feeling super horny and DTF, but your partner isn't? First of all, remember that sex isn't something that is owed. As blunt as it is, you need to respect your partner's feelings and understand that no matter what you do for them, they don't owe you sex at all. Secondly, it's good to know each other's 'sex number'. No, I'm not referring to 69. Both of you should rate yourself out of 10 based on how sexual you are. Doing this gives you a clearer understanding of the issue and

improves mutual understanding of your sexual needs. Have a discussion and broaden the range of activities that can be considered sexual by the two of you. You'll be able to develop a middle ground where it's sexually satisfying for the partner that has higher libido, but not uncomfortable for the other. If your issue regarding incompatibility isn't about libido, but actual sexual activities then this strategy can also work. In extreme cases, if you and your partner are up for it, you could consider polygamy. As mentioned early on, I have no credibility when it comes to sex advice so this is all I've got.

3. **Prolonged stress** – In life, shit happens. When you're in a relationship, this doubles because when your partner goes through a tough time, you're going to be experiencing it too. While it's important that you are there for each other, sometimes the stress can become overwhelming. First of all, you need to identify the stressor – the root of the stress. Relationship stressors can include work-related stress, long-term mental illness and, in the future, maybe infertility or financial problems. Secondly, look at the nature of the problem. Does it affect one person primarily (work), or is it more equal in distribution (financial)? Is it external (family issues) or is it internal (injury)? If it affects your partner more than you, you may feel inclined to stick with them through this. That's a great mindset, but many people fail to realise that they have their own mental and physical limitations with help, leading to burnout. Remember that you are not your

partner's therapist. Dealing with an intimate partner's emotional load full-on in this way is dangerous.

So, what if the problem affects you both equally? In this case, you need to work as a unit with your partner. Stop thinking, 'what can I do to make it better for me?' and start thinking, 'what can we do to make it better for us?' Sometimes, solutions will require compromise. This may mean decreasing your weekly spending on coffee in order to save more money. Or cancelling holiday events that you want to go to because your partner is not emotionally up for it anymore. In general, to solve prolonged stress in a relationship, it's helpful to have a strong support network of supportive friends, family and possibly professional help.

4. **Loss of interest –** It's a terrifying thought that two people who were once so in love with each other could eventually just ... fall apart. Or that the things about you that your partner once considered beautiful they now see as ugly and just a distraction from their busy life. Don't be afraid if you feel a mutual loss of interest. So how does this happen? There are three main assumptions you can make that contribute to this problem: that you really know your partner, that you'll be with them for life and that they should see to all your needs. See, throughout a relationship, both you and your partner will change a lot from different experiences, and sometimes these changes will be undesirable to the other.

If things are meant to work out, they will. If not, they'll fall apart. If you and your partner are determined to keep this relationship going, there are things you can do to revive it and undo the boredom. First of all, you need to be satisfied with yourself and understand your partner is here to enhance your life, rather than complete it. Remember, high expectations will just set you up for more failure in this context. Next, don't let familiarity breed contempt. What that means is that you should still view your partner as the amazing person that you saw in your honeymoon period. Don't let the fact that you're used to them make them seem any less significant than as you first viewed them. Then, of course, you and your partner need to work on making the relationship fun again. Do more fun and unique dates - listen to the tracks you listened to in your honeymoon period or try something new in the bedroom. The possibilities are endless if you look around.

5. **Lack of communication** - Wow, newsflash - your partner isn't a mind reader! I've been through this, always hoping my partner could see how much emotional pain I was in at the very moment we were talking. But then at the same time, I appreciate my mental space. You're probably sick of me mentioning communication for the hundredth time here, but lack of communication is a pretty big killer for a relationship. The thing that normally happens during conflicts for poorly-communicating couples is silence. This silence could mean compliance, which seems to work to initially, but eventually snowballs. Then, it could be during an argument when the

compliant partner completely boils over and lashes out in a way never seen before. Now that's ugly. The silence could also be the response of an upset/unsatisfactory partner. That's called the silent treatment. It's incredibly frustrating when your partner just suddenly stops talking to you and when you ask them what's wrong, they don't tell you. It's passive-aggressively toxic and apart from making you feel like shit, it achieves absolutely nothing.

To fix this problem, first take a look at why people do this in the first place. It's very likely that they have either experienced the silent treatment as a child, and therefore has experienced its effectiveness first-hand, or have trouble expressing their feelings. Either way, you need to meet your partner with empathy, while still acknowledging to them that you dislike the silent treatment and how it makes you feel (more on confrontational skills in part 9). Don't blame yourself or retaliate. Seek a strong support network as you talk to your partner about this issue.

The list of issues you encounter in a relationship is pretty much endless. But these are five of the biggest problems you'll face when you get comfortable in the long haul. Even if you haven't encountered any problems yet, it's good to have preparation for the future. You never know what might happen.

Meet Me in the Ring!

I really dislike the common understanding people have of couple fights. On the outside, it looks like you're literally engaging in a verbal fistfight with your partner. But it's really crucial to remember that fights are not about you vs your partner, but rather **you two vs the problem.** As we saw above, issues will definitely arise in your long-term relationship. And while the long haul will leave you two scared, frustrated and intimidated, you can most definitely get through it.

You can never completely avoid fights in a relationship. But you can definitely make them beneficial. This is what we call a fair fight. Here are 11 ways to turn this painful part of a relationship into something that will promote personal growth and understanding:

1. **Don't fear conflict** – Like I said previously, fighting in a relationship isn't necessarily a bad thing, and you should be more concerned if you're not fighting at all. Problems will always arise in a relationship and if you think about it, at least fighting means you're addressing it. So, the first step of fighting fairly is for you and your partner to understand that fighting is normal and essential.

2. **Team up with your partner** – You know the phrase 'us against the world'? Well, in the context of fights this is especially important. Remember, fights should always be about solving the problem together as a couple. Never ever attack your partner as an individual. This can do a lot more harm than you think. More on abusive behaviour like this will be covered in The Silent Hand later on.

3. **Differentiate topic from issue** – Have you ever noticed that sometimes when you fight with the same person often, you slide back to a larger, reoccurring topic? For example, you and your partner might argue over different situations like paying bills, going overseas, buying gifts etc., but if you can look closely at how they end, you'll see they all lead to one single issue: money. That's the target to address when fighting fairly. The roots of the tree. Deal directly with the issue, and you'll stop fighting unnecessary proxy wars.

4. **Avoid downplaying the issue** – The worst thing you can do when your partner brings up an issue is to shake it off. If they believe it's an issue, you need to respect your partner and let them know you're listening to what they have to say, and that you'll do something about the problem. Ignoring a problem or saying, 'oh that's nothing,' won't make it go away. For you, being 10 minutes late to every date might not seem a big deal, but your partner may begin to feel annoyed about your lack of punctuality. It doesn't matter whether their query to you is something valid to you or not, you should still take time to listen and talk about it.

5. **Forget about mind reading** – Don't assume your partner can read your mind. Be as open as you can, even if your words won't be met with a positive response. Trust me, communicating everything is better than soothing the situation, which could come back and bite you in the ass because your partner finds out you were lying to them. At the

same time, don't try to read your partner's mind. Making assumptions will hurt you. Always encourage them to speak to you truthfully and to not hold back. Even if it might hurt you.

6. **Be attentive** – There are people that, when faced with unpleasant conflict, will sort of drift off. When I am hit with a barrage of homophobic comments from people, my excellent selective hearing will kick in. But that's just not going to help you. In one instance, the argument will continue endlessly, emotionally tiring your partner. You wouldn't want your partner to feel like that, right? Alternatively, lack of attention may make them end the conversation because they feel as though you don't care or want to listen to them.

7. **Never yell** – To raise your voice means you care more about being right than making things right. Yelling in an argument indicates that it is already unproductive, and no points are being heard or understood. Strong emotions can get in the way when it comes to fighting fair. Yelling, like personal attacks, are not only unproductive, but can hurt your partner greatly and can constitute as abusive behaviour.

8. **Don't make generalisations** – Phrases like 'you always' and 'you never' cut deep and are always emotionally-driven. Perhaps your partner just forgot to take the trash out three times out of one hundred, but on this fourth time, your angry

brain makes a montage of every single time they haven't. And like the media, your brain will cut out all of the times they have done the task correctly, creating the illusion that they're incompetent with the chore. When you use a generalisation, you can pretty much guarantee your partner will immediately come up with exceptions. This is waste of time and unproductive for your argument.

9. **Throw away your ego** - Ego can get in the way when it comes to fighting. It is the greatest barrier to fighting fair and to constructive progress. One way to surrender your ego is to take criticism constructively. I understand it can be hard to stomach it, especially if you're in the middle of a fight, but learn to filter out the useful things. In turn, if you need to talk to your partner about fighting, use language that is respectful and understandable. Another way to fight back the ego is to be honest and apologise when you're wrong. And how can you apologise? Well, I've got a whole segment on that for you later.

10. **Make a habit of compromise** - Finding something - anything - that you can compromise on during a fight will go a long way. It indicates that while you deserve to be heard and understood, you're not unwilling to make things right. Making a step towards compromise, no matter how small, can also allow your partner to follow suit. This builds up a middle ground that both of you can reference to indicate that you two are on the same team.

11. **Don't leave it unfinished** - Don't allow issues to stay unresolved for two long. The longer you two sit on it, the more often proxy wars will spawn, and the more built-up resentment will grow. Closure is the more important goal. Without sounding like you are just trying to avoid arguing, indicate to your partner that you're determined to solve the problem quickly and fairly.

To finish off, here's a phrase guide of things that will definitely make things worse, what to say instead and what to say that will directly help your situation. And remember, you better not use this guide as a way to smartly manipulate your partner into shutting up. Fights always happen for a reason and include sadness or frustration from one or both people. They're not just annoying little skirmishes that come with dating your partner. Every time you refer to this list, make sure you put your heart into really understanding why you would or wouldn't use those phrases. Don't be a piece of shit. If you aren't willing to listen to your partner, then don't bother being with them.

The aggravators work against your relationship because they're phrases that are insensitive and focus more on your own personal interests (whether it is being right or avoiding conflict), and demean your partner's feelings. They are also emotionally-charged phrases that can do a lot of damage. The replacements work around these phrases and say similar things that you want to say in the aggravator section, but in a much more civil and sensitive way. Replacements form the basis for criticism, so you can deliver what you need to say and work on a common ground by problem-solving. The diffusers tone down the atmosphere of the argument, which are helpful as they make you and your partner more open to hearing criticism and keener to fix things. They also remind your partner that you love them and genuinely want to improve the relationship.

Aggravators	Replacements	Diffusers
"Whatever."	"I understand this is upsetting for you."	"I'm starting to feel defensive."
"That's ridiculous!"		
"Oh, that's just great." (sarcasm)	"We need to work together."	"I'm sorry I made you feel ..."
"You never ..."	"I don't really understand ..."	"We were both wrong."
"You always ..."		
"Calm down!"	"I need you to stop yelling so I can understand you."	"Let's talk about a resolution."
"You're such a (slur)!"		"What if ..."
"Oh god, not this again."	"We need to fix this issue, or it'll keep coming up."	"I love you."
		"I miss you when we fight."
"I hate you!"	"I'm feeling ..."	

The Hardest Word

The most difficult word to say also happens to be the most healing word. There will always come a time where you realise that you are genuinely wrong. You might feel silly that there's a section here on how to apologise. Come on, it's only one word, how hard can it get? Well, trust me, this word can feel so heavy that you need some preparation in order to carry it and mean it. So, how can we say sorry? First of all, you need to defeat the most pervasive gremlin that closes your mouth when you try to apologise. That gremlin's called Ego.

Defeating the ego - Put it aside by acknowledging that apologising doesn't make you a lesser person. After all, everyone makes mistakes, and no relationship is perfect. What's more important, you being right or your relationship being healthy? Your ego will get in the way for a sincere and heartfelt apology as it fears that you'll be temporarily vulnerable. However, if your partner really loves you, they won't take advantage of this vulnerability, and will instead appreciate it. Reflect on what you are apologising for and what you did wrong.

Demonstrate that you are sorry - Find a moment in time that isn't full of distractions. If you found out you were wrong after a fight, immediately apologise when there's a pause in action. Maintain eye contact and be calm when you deliver your apology. Admit your mistakes and explain what you did wrong. Acknowledge that you've hurt your partner's feelings. Take full responsibility for their feelings, and don't use 'but' or anything that shifts blame on them for feeling upset. If you can't apologise immediately, you can also use a gift to supplement your apology. This is especially effective if it aligns with their love language.

Ask for forgiveness – Be mentally prepared for a 'no'. And if you do get a 'no', understand that your partner may not be ready to forgive you yet, and that's normal – especially if your mistake was especially heinous. They aren't obligated to forgive you, and you can't demand it from them. It will be hard for your partner to tell you this because they love you, so make sure you let them know you understand the difficulty they are facing in this situation and that you understand. When your partner does forgive you, do not take it for granted. Let them know your gratitude for their humility and patience.

Forgive yourself – At the same time, make sure you can forgive yourself. It's probably more difficult to do than to ask for forgiveness for someone else, but to do so is the ultimate act of humility for the relationship. Being in the right mindset and moving forward will benefit the relationship.

Commit to improvement – Apologies aren't the end of a conflict. It's only one step in the whole process of growth through fighting. The next thing you need to do is to show the sincerity of your apology and to show that you are worth their forgiveness. Commit to avoiding a mistake like this again. These have to be things that you and your partner can actually see and feel. Simply saying, "yeah, I won't do it again," is empty and meaningless. Actions speak louder than words.

There are some times where apologising *isn't* the right thing to do. If your partner demands an apology for any of the following things, then it's the sign of an unhealthy relationship:

- ❖ Your hobbies

- ❖ Your opinions (as long as they aren't hateful/offensive things)

- ❖ Your quirks

- ❖ Trivial mistakes

- ❖ Something you didn't do

- ❖ Feeling sad or having a negative emotion

- ❖ Expressing your needs

- ❖ Nothing

If you find yourself easily apologising for things that don't need to be apologised for, or you're apologising for no reason, yet your partner still demands it from you, then you may have a bigger problem to deal with.

The Way the Cookie Crumbles

Sometimes, the apology just won't do or the fight just won't resolve itself. Or the love just won't stay. It can be especially distressing when you figure out that a romantic relationship is doomed to fail. But hey, you got to remember, there's only really two possible ways for a relationship to end: you either die before it ends, or it ends before you die. I'm no good at maths, but I'm pretty sure that a relationship failing isn't unusual, right?

Despite break-ups scoring high on the list of things that feel unpleasant, it won't kill you. So, here's some ways we can deal with them better and even turn them into fuel for positive growth.

Preparing for the Inevitable

Many people consider breaking up months before they actually do. It takes time to emotionally stomach something like this. It doesn't matter who initiates the break-up, it could be mutual for all I know, but literally no one is 100% caught off guard during a break-up. So, here's how you can prepare yourself.

First of all, there are signs that a relationship is about to meet its end. While you may think 'of course a person knows they want to end a relationship, what are you, stupid?' In reality, a lot of people live in denial that things will get better. They may misdiagnose the situation as just a rough patch. There is definitely a difference between a relationship that can be fixed and one that needs to be abandoned.

There are four clues that a relationship that are in its final days. Once all four of these have become apparent to you, you'll know that it's time to leave:

1. **A lack of sex and affection** – This can also indicate a regular rough patch, but a relationship that is permanently damaged will see even the smallest patterns of affection (waving goodbye, kissing on the way out the door) disappear. Moreover, a relationship that is on the decline will suffer from this problem persistently over a long period of time. Sure, this can all be excused by daily distractions and stress, but back in the honeymoon days, these stressors still existed. The only thing that changed was that you and your partner no longer tried to make it work. The lack of physical affection also symbolises the lack of physical *attraction*. And if you're not attracted to them, then there's no romance.

2. **You no longer want to communicate** – You feel like you're running out of things to talk about with your partner. It might get to the point where they seem boring, and when trouble arises you find it difficult to communicate with them about it, despite it being easier so many months ago. Because of that, the relationship feels highly stressful and excuses are frequently made to decrease intimacy. This is one of the most obvious signs of a failing relationship because even regular rough patches don't do this much damage. The loss of communication already indicates that there's no connection between you and your partner.

3. **There's built-up resentment** – People embrace and accept each other's flaws in a relationship, but when the romance is dying this will change. Something that was once a cute quirk will turn into something that irritates you. In fact, both of you will find more and more annoying things about each other, and become more sensitive to these things. This will in turn increase fruitless fights that harm the bond between you and your partner. Increased resentment means your brain is linking together evidence that your partner is undesirable and that you should leave.

4. **You think about escape** – This is different to simply contemplating on giving up during a rough patch. When a relationship is ready to die, you'll genuinely feel trapped, and fantasies of leaving will occupy your mind in prolonged detail. You may even daydream about getting into a new relationship, and how much better life would be afterwards.

If these things describe how you feel right now, you may consider leaving your relationship. But only you know whether these signs are legit or not.

So, how do you mentally and physically prepare for a break-up? I've compiled a helpful checklist for you. If you really have decided that you want to leave, then take a look at this on the next page.

The Break-up Checklist

- ☐ **Do you have an idea what you'll be doing with your partner's memorabilia?** How will you deal with stuff that reminds you of them? Will destroying it (legally) make you feel better? Maybe the break-up is mutual and you may find that there's no need for you to do anything here really.

- ☐ **Do you have a strong support system?** Do you have friends and family who will be ready to support you when the break-up happens? Will they be able to offer help that focuses on your personal wellbeing, as opposed to biased opinions regarding possible relationship drama etc.?

- ☐ **Will you be fully independent?** Relationships usually cause people's lives to overlap financially, physically and emotionally. After the break-up, will you be able to regain independence? Do you have a place to live, your own money etc.?

- ☐ **Are you ready to deal with changes in circles?** Our circles are comparable to nets. When you pull at one end of the net, the nearby loops distort with it. Are you ready for circles to be affected by the break-up, even negatively?

- ☐ **Do you have a positive outlook?** I get that it's hard, but having a positive outlook is needed in order to allow healing. Do you believe that the break-up isn't the end of the world? Do you have faith that you will move on with your life?

Doing the Do

Alright now, let's get to the actual break-up. Let's say you've read this whole chapter until here. It's important that you do, because all the knowledge above can help minimise the pain of a break-up. Despite that, it will still leave a lasting impression. Think of it more like pressing a branding iron against your skin. You feel terrified before it happens. When the branding iron actually brands you, the pain can be very overwhelming and intense. In that moment, that's the life you know and you start to crave the sweet release of death. But almost immediately, the iron is lifted off your skin and leaves an ugly burn mark. Guess what, over the course of time, it will fade. Not into oblivion, but there will be a day where it will be nothing but a faint shape. By then, you'd still remember the unpleasant memory, but it wouldn't hurt as much anymore.

So, with that unnecessarily long analogy, I'd like to offer you the rundown of how it actually works.

There are many reasons you'd want to terminate a romantic relationship with someone. Perhaps you've fallen out of love, and neither of you have the desire to get it back. Or maybe your partner has made a mistake that you can't forgive. Or maybe you've finally had enough of their toxic ways. Whatever your reason, breaking up can cause a lot of different emotions – sadness, anger, guilt, relief. Our main goal as a breaker-upper is to end a relationship as maturely and peacefully as possible. No matter what your partner did, we need to be the bigger person. In movies, we see people slashing tyres and breaking windows after a break-up. It looks exhilarating but seriously, this behaviour won't work in real life and will only paint you as an emotionally immature and crazy person for future love interests.

Researchers have drawn up four main strategies used by people to break-up. These were:

1. Positive tones, which reduce a partner's negative feelings.

2. Openness, which clearly communicates the reason for a break-up.

3. Avoidance/withdrawal, which decreases contact with the partner.

4. Manipulation, which refers to using break-up strategies that involve deceit or a third party.

Frequency doesn't necessarily correlate with effectiveness though. The last two strategies are especially ineffective when the goal is a civil break-up. So, as a breaker-upper, here's what you should do:

- Find time to talk face-to-face with your partner. Make sure there are no distractions.

- Tell your partner that you don't regret spending time with them.

- Honestly convey to them what you're feeling and the reasons for breaking up.

- Emphasise some good things that came from the relationship.

- ❖ Avoid blaming your partner or hurting their feelings.
- ❖ Convince your partner that the break-up would be better for both parties.

Remember, even if you feel your partner is irredeemable, be the bigger person. Be kind.

The Silent Hand

<u>Abuse</u> is a vague word. So many people in this world think they know exactly what it means, but they don't. When I say 'abuse', you may think of an angry man punching holes in the wall. Or you might see a mother hitting her kids relentlessly. But abuse is actually a very broad term and can be hard to pinpoint for many victims and even abusers, romantically, platonically and domestically. On the other hand, it's easy for more emotionally in-tune people to see it in other people. That's why, if those that you trust are talking to you about it, then it's best to listen.

The Ingredients of an Abusive Relationship
Not all the signs are obvious. In order to identify an abusive relationship, you need to stay away from media stereotypes. More often than not, many victims don't recognise signs of abuse that have been there all along, simply because it doesn't seem severe enough to be 'counted' as abuse. The thing is ... there's no scale of severity for abuse. **Abuse is abuse.**

Remember the red flags we covered earlier? Some of them are also signs of an abusive partner, but just to make it clearer, I'm going to explicitly state the actual key signs. They can be broadly classified into five main categories:

Possessiveness – Your partner checks in on you way too much for your comfort and gets angry when they slightly lose sight of you, or when you choose to go against anything they say.

Jealousy – Your partner constantly accuses you of being unfaithful and flirty. They attempt to isolate you from other people like friends and family. This ties quite closely with possessiveness.

Put-downs – Your partner constantly puts you down and attacks your intelligence, appearance, mental health and/or capabilities. They put the blame on you for every issue in a relationship, and constantly remind you that no one else would want you.

Threats – Your partner intimidates you by breaking things and slamming doors. They also threaten violence against people you know.

Physical and sexual violence – Your partner enacts violent behaviour on you or forces you into sexual activities that you don't consent to. They may also be violent to your pets, friends or family members.

As you see, the stereotype of abuse being physical isn't correct. Physical abuse is only one of the five key signs.

Push and Pull

The most useless and disrespectful piece of advice you can ever give to someone who suspects they're being abused is 'you should just leave'.

Seriously, you might as well give them the finger. If it *was* that easy to leave, you would never hear any stories of abusive relationships because they'd all be over within seconds. If you still don't understand, it's okay. This is, unfortunately, one of the few things in life that you can't fully comprehend unless you've experienced it first-hand.

Remember the whole idea of infatuation? It distorts your view of a person. It's not that you completely forget all their negatives, but they feel less important to you. You'd rather focus on their positives, because that's what gives you your dose of oxytocin. That is one of the reasons why it's so hard for victims to leave. Even if they know deep down it's wrong and harmful for them, their less sensible, hormone-run brain doesn't think so. You'll also see this happen after regular break-ups.

Victims in abusive relationships experience this cognitive dissonance as a sort of 'push and pull', where in one instance you'll feel certain, but in another, not so much. Typically, straight after a traumatic event a victim will be able to fully acknowledge that they are in a toxic relationship. They will start thinking about leaving. But then, the abuser may apologise or show affection to the victim. This will confuse the victim, causing them to question their sanity. It's sad, but this is just one of the psychological tricks that abusers play. These tricks can have long term damage on people.

Abuse can happen in many forms, but the real damage comes from the underlying psychology. It's human instinct for us to get away from harm. If I'm a neighbour you don't know well, and I were to smack you across the face or take your wallet without saying anything, I'm sure you'd want to get the hell outta there, right? But partners aren't strangers, or people that would hurt us randomly. Well, they're not *supposed* to. We know relationships are *supposed* to be caring and nurturing. Your partner is *supposed* to protect you from harm and have your best interest in mind. But that doesn't always happen. It's this type of expectation vs reality that breaks a victim.

Mental break. I once saw this interesting little political cartoon, where there was a man standing on one end of a wooden plank. On the other was a small crowd that looked terrified of that man's menacing stare. The twist? The plank was balanced over a cliff. The lone man was standing on the edge jutting out into the abyss, while the crowd was on the solid ground. If the crowd was to step off the plank, the man would plunge to his death. Yet, the crowd stayed put and allowed themselves to submit to that one man. I find this rather similar to the abuser vs victim situation. Victims fail to realise that they actually have a lot more options than they think. They can easily step off the plank and get away (okay, I know it's not that simple, but you get the gist). After all, abusers are like parasites; toxic entities that require some sort of host to thrive. While lacking in actual control (what are they going to do, freeze you with ice powers?) their strength lies in their effective manipulative and toxic behaviour. After all, psychology is pretty much a person's weak spot. Break a bone, and it'll heal in a few months. But break a mind, and it might never mend.

So let's take a closer look at the emotional strategies that abusers use to trap a victim. When you read these, you may find out that some of them are happening in your own relationship. If that's the case, don't panic. Use this as a way to validate your experiences and convince yourself that you absolutely have to leave.

Emotional Blackmail (e.g. "If you leave this relationship, I'm going to kill myself!"; "If you call the police, I'll hurt your family!") - Causes guilt, fear and obligation in the victim.

Silent Treatment (as seen previously in this chapter) (e.g. Giving an apathetic response or none at all; withdrawing affection and attention to the victim.) - Denies the victim an opportunity to negotiate after conflict, therefore allowing the abuser a position of power and uncertainty.

Love Bombing (e.g. "No one else will love you"; showing intense affection over a short period of time.) - Wins a victim over, and also restarts the 'Cycle of Abuse'.

Gas Lighting (e.g. "I didn't do any of that, you're crazy."; "It wasn't that serious.") - Causes a victim to question the validity of their own perception of the abuser and situation.

The Origin of the Abuser

Now you may be wondering one thing: why do people abuse? Surely, we as a species that is built in with altruistic instinct, wouldn't have such a big problem with intrapersonal abuse, right? There are actually a few obvious factors of an abuser.

A person may be abusive because:

1. **They have difficulty dealing with hurt** - This is something that normally starts in childhood. An abuser who was raised by cotton-wrapping parents never learns how to deal with things that don't go their way.

For example, Johnny has a tantrum when another kid at day care takes his train. And what do his parents do? Instead of teaching him to stand his ground or maybe to share, they buy him a new train, no questions asked. Later in life, trains are replaced by homework, job opportunities and partners. Johnny is simply so used to everyone making things right for him that Johnny has failed to develop any coping mechanisms or resilience for when things don't go his way. Even though his parents, teachers and peers could help him, he'd eventually reach a point in his life where he has to open his eyes and deal with crap himself. If he gets into a relationship and his partner upsets him, he will adopt an unhealthy mindset and take out his frustration and anger on them. A difficulty in dealing with hurt voids him of healthily communicating with his partner over issues.

2. **They feel entitlement** – There are certain people in the world who believe they have a right to not be hurt or embarrassed. While that sounds like a normal human thing, entitlement refers to an almost unconditional hatred and avoidance of hurt, to the point where the person would sacrifice other people's needs and feelings because they believe that they deserve special treatment.

So Johnny did pretty well in school because his parents could afford a lot of resources and put him in a good college. There, he also makes a lot of friends who admire him for his performance. When he finally meets his girlfriend things start off fine. But when they argue, Johnny takes it particularly sensitively, and feels incredibly defensive. Even though he knows during the argument that his girlfriend is right, he still fails to acknowledge it or apologise, because he knows he's an exceptional guy (as said by everyone) and compromising would hurt his ego. Therefore, Johnny opts to use manipulative tricks on his girlfriend after the argument to make her feel as though she's wrong, despite that being untrue.

3. **They lack empathy** – Empathy is a word that gets mixed up with 'sympathy' a lot, so many people just assume they're interchangeable and both mean feeling a degree of care for another person going through negative emotions. That's not correct at all. Empathy is the ability of someone to understand another person's viewpoint and feelings. It could be positive or negative. Sometimes, an abuser may simply lack empathy and don't understand that their behaviours are harming their victims. Other times, they see from their victim's perspective, but in a distorted light.

    Our boy Johnny has some degree of empathy, but no generosity, which is an important ingredient for positive empathy. Therefore, he sees that his girlfriend is scared of him, but interprets it as her creating distance from him. Johnny then, of course, feels hurt by that, and punishes her even more in order to try and correct that behaviour.

4. **Unaddressed trauma** – Years and years of psychology research has shown us that many abusers have been abused themselves. Many of these people may have been brought up

in homes where they experience violence, neglect or sexual assault. This becomes unresolved trauma that they carry with them through to adulthood. If unaddressed, these people frequently learn that these behaviours are completely normal and will have no problem inflicting it on others. They will also have trouble forming healthy relationships with others.

Although Johnny lived a comfortable life sheltered from everything and did well in school, his parents pressured him greatly about it. They frequently spoiled him with material goods, but then neglected him for long periods of time, and only showed affection when he performed well at school. When he didn't do well, his parents would punish him severely and often violently. This left Johnny with lots of emotional scars growing up. He also interpreted his parent's behaviour as how he should act. Therefore, he will also act violently towards his girlfriend and show little attention to her unless he is showering her with material gifts.

Just a quick note, if you are suffering from abuse, do not **ever** attempt to 'heal' your abuser. Although you may care about them, especially if they have been through a cycle of abuse, you must understand that it is probably a futile act. Even if you are a trained psychologist yourself, it is always unwise for you to remain in an abusive relationship with a person while spending time and effort on helping them. There's a reason why many psychologists refrain from treating people they are close to. If you truly do want to help them (and help yourself heal from scars), I highly recommend you consult a therapist.

The study of abusive behaviour; its pattern of evolution based on human development, and how it renews itself down generations, is a very interesting topic in psychology. I could go on about it, but this book intends to cover as many areas of romance as I can, so I can't just babble on about how abuse happens and whatnot. If you are interested, I recommend browsing articles on Psychology Today, which is a fantastic website run by psychologists, but formatted so that the language and concepts are understandable for regular people.

Oh, and one last thing. Always, always remember that it isn't the end. You may feel trapped now, but please remember that bad things have their place. It takes a lot of courage to take a step forward. Take your time. But never give up. The amount of help you actually have can surprise you. Trust me, I know.

Alright, now moving on. Literally.

Get Over It

Break-ups leave people in shambles. I think the best way I've ever heard someone describe it was a caller I talked to on Lifeline. I remember her saying something along the lines of, "A break-up is a form of loss, and it is something that requires you to process. You need to process the grief."

Great words indeed. The thing you're mourning isn't just the relationship, but all the expectations, hopes, dreams and memories you've developed. And let me tell you, it hurts so much. But, like all losses, it is something that can be improved, if you let it.

The Five Stages of Grief

To learn how to get over a break-up, let's first reimagine it as the loss it really is. And what better way to do it than to use the 'Five Stages of Grief' model?

Stage 1: Denial – Your ears probably heard it. And your emotions have most likely processed it, that's why there's tears and snot all over your face. But yet, you don't believe it. Your heart still thinks that the relationship is still there, and you may still fantasise about an alternate reality where things work out. You're still a little drugged up from the love hormones. You feel upset, but you fail to comprehend why. There are some people that will actually be stuck in this first stage for a long, long time. Their habit of denying the truth means they struggle to accept their feelings for healing.

Stage 2: Anger – Afterwards, you feel an intense anger at everything. This could be directed at your ex ('How can you do this?'), yourself ('Why am I so stupid?'), or life in general ('Why does this keep happening to me?'). In this stage, you'll feel extra resentful about almost everyone and everything that have even the slightest connection to your relationship. For many that feel overcome by this stage, they will send out spiteful messages to them or even vandalise their property.

Stage 3: Bargaining – After the anger resides, a person will reach the next stage. This stage can also be reimagined as a person going through a second, slightly different denial. You'll start to ask yourself a lot of 'what ifs' and look at possible strategies that will undo the loss, sometimes even ludicrous ones. Those that are stuck in the bargaining stage find themselves making promises and deals they cannot keep in order to fix something that is beyond repair. They may even consult supernatural forces in order to make things right.

Stage 4: Depression – When the realisation that the break-up really is irreparable finally hits, the depression settles in. Coincidentally, this is a time where the love hormones completely wear off and you're back to plain, unstable reality (that is perceived, anyways). If you've just terminated an especially long relationship, this adjustment may feel especially hard. Single people that have been single for a long time get used to it mentally and physically, and even develop tools to allow themselves to continue while being open to relationship prospects. You, on the other hand, would have been so used to company and constant oxytocin highs that this change may force you to relearn the world as you know. People are commonly stuck in this stage, where they start to rely on alcohol or other substances as a coping mechanism. They will also feel a persistent hopelessness and wonder if they will ever move on.

Stage 5: Acceptance – But of course, there's always a light at the end of a tunnel. Usually, it will take time, but you'll know when you're here. One day, you'll wake up and feel at peace with the loss. It doesn't mean you won't feel sad about it anymore, but it means that you no longer attach guilt and anger to yourself and your ex. You'll develop a mature, detached hindsight of the situation. It means acknowledging that it's now history, and it's time to get on with life.

This isn't necessarily linear and set in stone. Some people find themselves stuck for an especially long time in certain stages. Others blaze right through their break-up with little down time. Some people get very close to acceptance but then relapse. Maybe there are people that need external assistance to get through certain stages. The point is, everyone goes through it differently, and don't be afraid to ask for help. If you feel like you will never move on from this, then it probably means you're still in a stage of grief. That's okay though, you'll get there eventually.

Moving On

Alas, life's a one-way ticket. Even if you don't want to move, everything around you will, so it's best not to get left behind. Actually, scratch that. It's literally impossible to get left behind. Have you ever been in a period of time where you felt very low and unmotivated? Yet, time still went forward, so you felt yourself literally *dragged* through life? Well, the thing about getting dragged is that eventually you will find enough strength to start walking on your own again. So, when the loss of a relationship puts you into this period, you will find strength eventually.

There's no foolproof plan to healing. There are many factors involved, such as the nature of the break-up and your own emotional strength. Notice that I am not writing a step-by-step procedure, rather, a sprinkle of tips for you to listen to, or not. Either way, the only thing that will definitely fix a break-up is time. Here are 10 good tips to get you moving on to stage 5:

1. **Cease all contact** - You'll be tempted to stalk them on everything, but don't do it. Your healing period after a break-up requires you to have some space. Don't even look at their social media. Seeing images of them will most likely trigger you to think about your relationship, and if you think a lot about your past relationship, it'll be harder for you to move on. Only consider contacting them again after you know you're completely mentally healed. It may take years but that's reality.

2. **Get rid of mementos** - I personally do not advise burning all the things they gave you. Or packing it all into a bag and dumping it in front of their house. For some things, if you really want to, you can donate or sell. But if you aren't a fan of throwing things away, you can keep them all in a place out of reach. In the future, when you've healed, you can probably look at it again but, for now, your priority is to completely

erase this person from your life. Creating an ex-free environment can also mean tiny changes, whatever helps. When they leave, you'll be surprised to know just how much your life has been affected by them. But that's okay though, because even though it may be daunting and difficult to remove everything, you eventually will. For me, I even had to stop watching a TV show because my ex used to watch it with me.

3. **Bring up your break-up productively** - It's therapeutic to talk about your break-up with people. On the other hand, some people don't like talking about it at all. It's up to you, I guess. But if you do want to talk, make sure it's productive. Excessive shit-talk will get you nowhere. It may feel good, but it goes nowhere and just amplifies unwanted post-break-up emotions like anger, resentment; that type of stuff. Instead, it's better to discuss with your friends what went wrong with both of you, and how you can use this experience to ensure future relationships will be better.

4. **Don't think about 'friends' yet** - If your break-up was relatively peaceful (the keyword is *relatively*, break-ups are devastating), then you two may have discussed the prospect of remaining friends afterwards. Sounds good, but now isn't the time to promise them that. That's because you really can't tell. On the day of one of my break-ups, I was like 'hell yeah'. Then, a whole day later, I was like 'hmm maybe not'. And my response will probably change again in a few

months. Leave this decision till after you're emotionally stable again. And don't feel horrible if in the end you don't want to. It doesn't make you a bad or uncivil person.

5. **Be safe with coping** - Everyone copes with trauma differently. Some people cry and watch sad movies. Others drink a bit. Whatever you do, stay safe, especially if you're the kind that uses substance as a coping mechanism. Relatively 'unhealthy' coping mechanisms will provide temporary relief but will make you feel way worse afterwards. This is because you can alter your psychology through foreign chemicals, and we all know messing around adding chemicals to your brain isn't a good idea in the long run. It may even increase your dependency on the said substance. Instead, opt for coping mechanisms that aren't destructive, such as exercising and art. If you really want to drink or smoke, at least make sure you're in a safe environment with trustworthy friends who can stop you once you've had enough.

6. **Get a distraction** - With your romantic circle gone, it's best for you to focus your time on your two other circles - friends and family. Spending time with them helps to remind you that you're still loved. Going out and doing stuff with people will definitely beat being all sad and lonely at home, trust me. As you get older, you'll realise that support networks are absolutely vital when it comes to dealing with your romantic circle.

7. **Keep the break-up low-key** - I remember talking a lot about social media and its role in a relationship. Like I said, the more online-involved you guys were, the more you have to deal with when it ends. So, refrain from publicising your break-up and give you and your ex some privacy. You'll be embarrassed later if you write a 1,000-word Facebook status about it. And not to be blunt, but literally no one on your timeline is going to care so save your energy.

8. **Don't date again until you're emotionally ready** - Forget the whole 'rebound' thing. It's not healthy at all to do the dating equivalent of 'Hair of the Dog' (a myth that drinking while hungover fixes your hangover). Right after a break-up, your mind is especially vulnerable and needs to heal. This healing is best done by taking the focus away from romance for a while. Additionally, you could be easily taken advantage of because your emotions are not in check. This will make you susceptible to toxic relationships and ultimately damage you even more. So, just swear off dating for now. Trust me, once you feel better, dating will be back to normal.

9. **Don't retaliate** - This isn't a music video. Planning 'revenge' with your friends against your ex really shows your immaturity. In the end, it will also fuel spite between you and them. While it may be tempting, especially if they treated you poorly, you need to be the bigger person. People only heal post-break-up by minimising the negative emotions associated with it. And of course, vengeance is a negative

emotion. Instead of using your brain power to come up with revenge, use it to focus on your own healing.

10. **Don't blame yourself** – Especially if your ex left you because you did something 'wrong'. People always think of break-ups as a struggle for a person to leave an unhappy relationship and then thriving afterwards, but not everyone sees the other side. When you're the person being dumped for making a mistake, you may experience intense, crushing guilt. It's easy to descend into self-hate. But remember, break-ups require two people. You can't solely be the problem. Use an outside perspective and try and think of the problem from both sides. It might be difficult, but remember that mistakes aren't permanent, and you have the ability to avoid them next relationship. Forgive yourself and move on. Your ex wasn't perfect.

Like I said before, these are tips, not a procedure. You'll most likely do something different every time, but those above can help you a lot. For me, I feel a particularly strong connection to this. Let me share a dose of wisdom on healing that comes 100% from my own life. Whether it will help you, I don't know, but I hope it can make you understand that healing actually happens, and I'm not just a walking, talking 'top 10' clickbait article.

Only until my face was pressed into my friend's lawn, with alcohol- and sweat-soaked clothes, my body too heavy to move, did I know that I'd had enough. Not just enough to drink, but enough time to think. Right in this very moment of rock bottom, where the branding iron had just settled into my skin, I found light. I finally understood. Break-ups don't have to be wrecking balls in your life that weaken your will as you go on. This wasn't just something I wanted to be true, this was something that I NEEDED to be true. So, I decided to make it happen. Immediately, I gathered everything that reminded me of that particular ex and stored it in a box. I had to remove them from my life completely. Every time my mind drifted towards the memory of the break-up, or the last few years together, I'd snap out of it. It took some practice, but after a while, I realised this was doing me more good than when I just let my depressing thoughts spiral out of control after the break-up. I had two more things that I knew I needed to work on.

Firstly, I needed to stop being a victim. As strange as it sounds, self-victimisation is simply a by-product of ego. Why? Because if you accept that you're a victim, it also means that you accept that there are external circumstances that are causing your suffering. While that is true, can you really move on if you continually tell yourself that the world is against you? So, I immediately stopped thinking of myself as a broken mess. There was no need for me to rely on substances to prove the point that I was emotionally-damaged and relied on dangerous coping methods to further the narrative of my demise. I took a break from all my unhealthy coping mechanisms. As soon as I told myself that I was no longer a victim, I realised that everyone else's views of me had never changed in the first place. It turned out that the only person I was trying to convince about my tortured life was none other than me.

Next, I needed to love myself. With our built-in altruism, it's so easy for us to forget about ourselves. The crushing hand of society feeds off your feelings of self-dissatisfaction, and a stress of pleasing others, even if you don't want to. You have to agree that our generation seems to have a thing for self-deprecating humour right? On the surface, it seems like a humbler alternative to laughing at other people, but deep inside there's a sweeping bout of low self-esteem. And as someone that was born with low self-confidence, I found myself especially vulnerable to self-hate. As you can imagine, after my ex left me I was at a point where I couldn't even reason why I was worth being alive. However, I knew that I had to change, because if I kept telling myself that I was a horrible person and didn't deserve love, there was no way I could move on. So I actively shot down any self-doubting thoughts, and also stopped making self-deprecating jokes. What I practised wasn't egoism at all. As C.S. Lewis said, "humility is not thinking less of yourself, but thinking of yourself less".

So with these things, I found myself feeling a little lighter, happier and more at peace. I know it's easier said than done, but the thing is, it only works if you actually do it.

Surprising Benefits of Losing Love

Just as I decided to turn to positivity after a break-up instead of letting myself spiral into misery, you can too. Remember, break-ups aren't the end of the world. In Australia, we have certain trees that literally need a fire to raze the entire forest into the ground before the heat can help their seeds open and germinate the forest floor. And just like that, we can find benefits in the wake of the relationship destruction. Don't believe me? Read on.

For those that have endured an abusive relationship, a break-up is a second chance, or a rehab in a way. Years of abuse feel way worse than a 10-minute break-up. Of course, as we have learnt, it's not that simple, but a break-up is definitely a ray of hope. Also, a break-up is a bit of a diagnostic test that can give you an indication of yourself. It gives you alone time. No, not just time for you to lie on your bed and browse on your phone, but REAL alone time. The diagnosis isn't necessarily about your problems, even if the break-up wasn't entirely your fault. It helps you create better skills to avoid situations like this from happening again. It may also improve your ability to read potential partners. And of course, if it really was your problem, the diagnosis will tell you how to be a better partner.

I'm sure you've heard of post-traumatic stress disorder (PTSD). It's a psychological condition that people experience after suffering through traumatic events. Symptoms of PTSD include anxiety, panic attacks and depression, which are commonly 'triggered' through things that remind the person of the traumatic event. While trauma may have been short-term, PTSD normally lasts for a much, much longer time. But what if I told you that you can actually use trauma for the better?

Two psychologists in the 90s – Richard G Tedeschi and Lawrence G Calhoun – proposed the idea that humans who have undergone traumatic events can develop a positive psychological change out of it. Coined as post-traumatic growth (PTG), the two psychologists suggested that the mental resilience of humans can surpass simply healing after trauma, even reaching a higher level of functioning than before. Of course, over time there have been many scientists that have disputed the legitimacy of PTG, but I personally find it valid. If you don't believe in it, that's alright, it's up to you. But in case you do, stay with me.

Post-traumatic growth isn't something you have to immediately jump to. For many people that have just dealt with something like this, it's difficult for them to even imagine that things can get better. But after you've taken sufficient time to slow down and process these negative feelings, you'll find PTG possible. Here are some common traits that PTG develops for some people, not necessarily romance-related:

1. Forgiveness
2. A recognition of strength
3. Resilience
4. Greater compassion
5. Sense of purpose
6. Deepened connections to others

7. Appreciation for life

PTG is most definitely something that can be fostered, the only thing that you have to do to make sure it happens is to know that you can. That's it. Professional help is also available, but not every professional agrees in the existence of PTG, just putting it out there.

So, it's been a really long chapter, and not a particularly fun one compared to the previous chapters. If you are reading this because you need some help after a break-up, I just want to say that I'm very proud of you and you've been doing well so far. As you've learnt, break-ups aren't the end of the world, and it is absolutely possible for you to bounce back, and even get higher than you've ever been before. With a strong support network from friends and family, you'll thrive. Also, don't forget your strongest supporter: yourself!

But alas, this book's purpose isn't to provide commentary on trauma, heartbreak and sadness. Most of you are here because you want to learn how to find love! So, I'm going to avoid ending this book with the 'break-up' section, because, while the last few chapters have been relatively chronological, I don't want you to think that losing love is the endgame for the relationship process, because that's not always the case. To stay true to the book's title, let's move on back to all the fun, lovey-dovey stuff, shall we?

Part 9

Manuals and More

Not going to lie, there has been a LOT of theory in this book. I've also put out some step-by-step procedures, but they're more of your general stuff, such as how to get a date and say sorry. But let me tell you, the little things are just as important as the big things. This chapter is going to be the icing while the previous chapters were your raw ingredients (sorry for all the cake analogies, I promise this will be the last one). The advice here will help you to become a more attractive, romantic, and generally more desirable partner. Of course, most of these are just random useful skills that can be transferred to other contexts, but being a functional and likeable human being is normally a requirement for every single eligible bachelor/bachelorette on the planet.

For easy reading, I've separated this chapter into three main sections:

1. **Grooming and Appearance**

2. **Food and Lifestyle**

3. **People and Relationships**

So without further ado, and with generous research from other experts, I present you what I believe are the sixteen most important skills to have in order to be a successful lover.

Grooming and Appearance

If animals choose their mate based on the best fur colour, biggest horns and most exquisite dance moves, you don't need to cry 'shallow' when your date considers your appearance. There's no need to stress over outfits really. Have fun discovering your own aesthetic and style. Of course, there will still be some unwritten rules that are good to know.

Decoding Dress Code

I'm sure we've all received invitations to events that specify dress code. Most of the time, it's a no-brainer. Wear a suit or a fancy dress to a wedding. Wear swimmers to a pool party. You get the gist. But sometimes, there are people that go above and beyond with their planning invitations, and write dress codes that just make you think 'what the hell does all this mean?' Well don't worry, this quick guide will help you decode all that language and save you from embarrassment. Fun fact, even these terms may change based on context of the function so have fun.

Code	Typical clothing
Black Tie	Tuxedo (hello, black tie?), long gown
Business formal	Pantsuits, regular suit and tie, tailored dress
Business casual	Blazer, pencil skirt, slacks, collared shirt
Casual	Jeans, sneakers, jean jackets

How to Tie a Tie

One of the most popular Google searches ever. This shows you that there a certainly a lot of tie-wearers, and a lot of tie-wearers that have no idea what on earth they're doing. So here are a few common techniques.

Four-in-hand knot
Easy self-releasing asymmetrical tie.

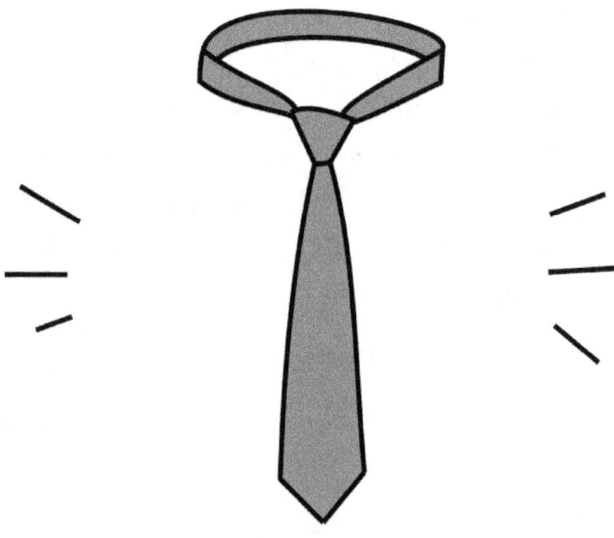

1. Drape necktie around your collar, thick end on the right.
2. Thick end goes over the narrow end.
3. Thick end goes back under the narrow end.
4. Thick end goes over narrow end again.
5. Thick end wraps up and over neck loop.
6. Thick end then goes through loop at the front.
7. Pull down on thick end to tighten and slide knot to adjust.

Windsor knot
Wide symmetrical tie.

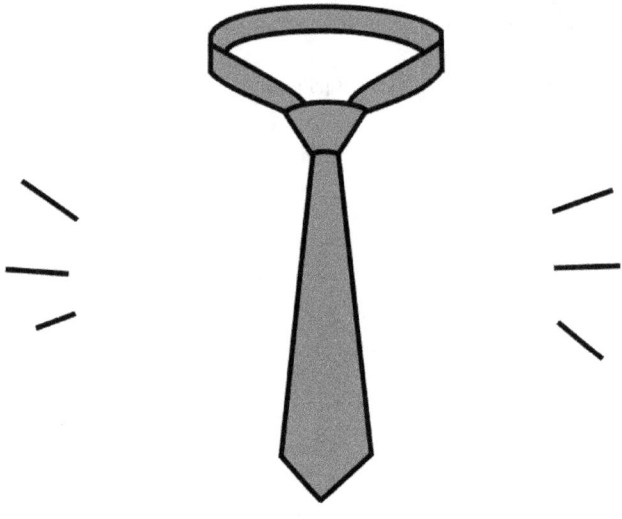

1. Drape the necktie over your collar, thick end on the right.
2. Thick end goes over narrow end.
3. Thick end goes up neck loop from the back.
4. Thick end goes over the front to the left.
5. Thick end goes behind narrow end to the right.
6. Thick end goes up over neck loop.
7. Thick end goes down into neck loop and then back out to the right.
8. Thick end goes across narrow end to the left.
9. Thick end goes up behind neck loop.
10. Thick end goes over and down into loop at the front.
11. Pull down on thick end to tighten and slide knot to adjust.

Trinity knot

Fancy triangular tie with 3-way symmetry.

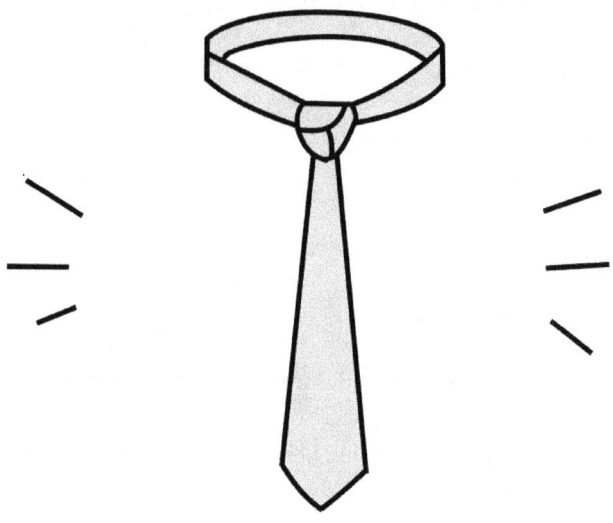

1. Drape necktie around your collar, thick end on the left.
2. Narrow end goes over thick end.
3. Narrow end wraps up the back of neck loop.
4. Narrow end goes over neck loop down to the left.
5. Narrow end goes under thick end to the right.
6. Narrow end goes over neck loop.
7. Narrow end goes down over the neck loop to the left.
8. Narrow end wraps across thick end and up the back of neck loop.
9. Narrow end goes down front loop.
10. Narrow end goes under thick end.
11. Narrow end goes up and into loop from step 9.
12. Tighten and tuck in narrow end to the left.

Eldredge knot

Eccentric and complex tie with semi-symmetrical triangles.

1. Drape necktie over your collar, thick end on the left.
2. Narrow end goes over thick end.
3. Narrow end goes back under thick end to the right.
4. Narrow end goes up over neck loop.
5. Narrow end goes down into neck loop to the left
6. Narrow end goes across thick end and back up into neck loop from behind.
7. Narrow end goes over and down neck loop from left and under thick end.
8. Narrow end goes over thick end and throw loop from step 7.
9. Pull narrow end to tighten.
10. Narrow end goes over neck loop and down into left from behind.
11. Narrow end goes over neck loop and behind neck loop on the right.
12. Narrow end goes under neck loop, across thick end, and into loop from step 11.
13. Pull narrow end to tighten.
14. Tuck narrow end into the left.

How to Roll Up your Sleeves

You may be thinking, really? Why the hell would you need a tutorial on how to roll up sleeves? Well, to my guys and gals out there who like to wear long-sleeve shirts, the way you roll your sleeves makes all the difference. Neatly-rolled sleeves give you a lot more class than bunching them up like a child would. Also, rolled sleeves makes your arms look more attractive and toned. It's common sense.

There are a lot of other sleeve rolls you can also do out there, but unlike ties, they are all very similar. The one that I've featured in this book is the Italian or Master, which is more popular for style purposes.

1. Unbutton your cuff and flip your cuff inside out.

2. Pull the cuff to just below your elbow. Don't fold; just turn the sleeves inside out as you go.

3. Fold up the bottom of the inside-out portion until you see just a little bit of the inside-out cuff.

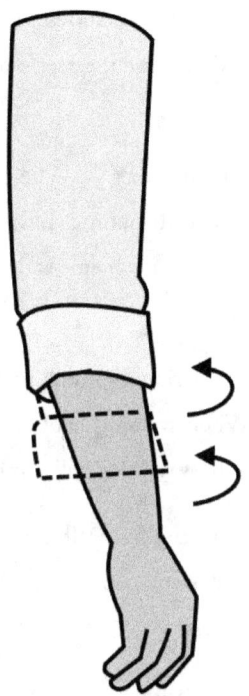

How to Walk in Heels

For the beginner heel-wearers, it can be quite daunting. No human is used to walking around on their toes for hours. It takes lots of practice, but you'll be looking elegant and slaying in no time.

Choose shoes that fit – With any shoes in general, walking will be difficult if they don't fit. Make sure the heels you choose aren't too big or too small.

Put down heel first and then toes – When wearing flat shoes like sneakers, we are accustomed to putting down the whole foot at once. However, when wearing heels, it's better to walk heel to toe. This will make you look more natural.

Take small steps – This is perhaps something that many amateur heel-wearers don't realise. When wearing heels, you need to reduce your stride. I learnt that the hard way. This will improve your balance.

Work your core – Apparently, walking in heels requires your abdominal muscles. Maintaining good core strength will improve your ability to walk or run in heels.

Have good posture – Heels will naturally make you lean forward, so if you hunch forward anymore, you'll look really awkward. Keep your back straight and even lean back a little for good balance.

Imagine a straight line when you walk – To walk more gracefully, look forward at your destination and imagine a straight line connecting you to it. It can serve as a guide while you walk. Much better than looking down at your feet.

The Colour Wheel

Colours deserve more credit than they're normally given. It's literally an art to figure out which colours go well with others and what meaning they all represent. The colour wheel is a fantastic tool that is used by all creative people alike: stylists, painters, and even web designers. So it's very strategic for you to get your hands on it. It will greatly improve the colour scheme of your style. This is a typical configuration of the colour wheel. If you can't see the colours here there are always plenty of resources online.

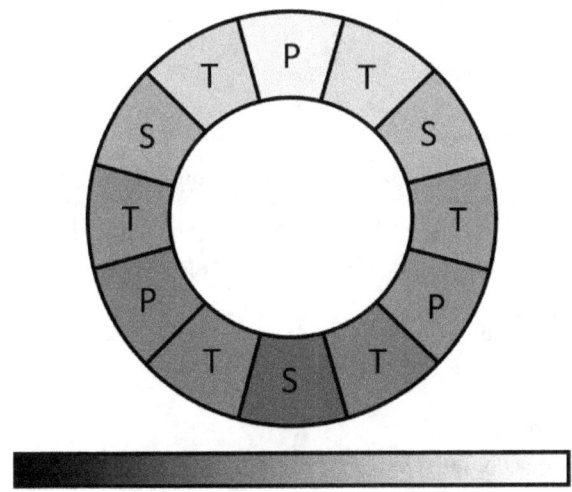

Primary, secondary and tertiary refers to how a certain shade is produced. The primary colours (yellow, red and blue) can't be made by mixing other colours, and every colour is derived from them.

Secondary colours are made by combining two primary colours. Tertiary colours are made by combining primary and secondary colours.

You've also got your 'warm' and 'cold' colour schemes. Warmer colours (red, orange, yellow) make things look smaller, and therefore a suitable for those that want to look slimmer. Cooler colours like blue, purple and green are soothing colours.

Neutral colours are the ones that look muted and plain. This includes black, white and beige. Despite their description, neutral colours aren't necessarily boring, and can look very classy and elegant.

So now you know what the colour wheel is, let's look at how it's applied to fashion.

Complementary colours
Complementary colours are obviously colours that look good when put together. They're normally directly opposite to each other on the wheel. This creates a stark contrast with a bold statement.

Example: Red and green, blue and orange, yellow and purple.

Analogous colours
An analogous colour scheme is one that uses two or three shades that are right next to each other on the colour wheel, meaning they blend well. This creates a very stylish look.

Example: Red, orange and yellow together.

Monochrome

This refers to just using one colour. It can be quite tricky to pull off, because you'll need to make sure the shade is consistent and you actually have the needed clothing items in that colour. However, monochrome looks pretty good. You can choose which colour you want based on the season and function.

Pattern

If you wear a piece of clothing that includes a print or pattern, it's best to make everything else plain. Too many patterns can become chaotic or confusing. Also minimise your accessories to make yourself look less clumsy.

Neutral Scheme

If you are ever unsure or want to be on the safe side, it's best to stick with neutral colours. As mentioned previously, these are perfect for looking elegant and classy. They're also quite versatile and will look good all year round, regardless of the function.

Manner and Lifestyle

It's said that actions are worth more than words. That's right. A lot can be said about you based on the things you do. The following guides will teach you certain skills that will definitely impress your partner and make them view you as a romantic and practical person.

Meal Etiquette

It's always the little things that are the most impressionable. Eating is a big part of human social bonding, so getting to know some unspoken rules about meal time will make you a better person. To make this all short and sweet, I've included some quick information on how to set up a table in a few different ways and how to arrange your cutlery at a restaurant.

Setting up a table

Learning how to set a table makes you seem like a highly organised and civilised person, and also makes dinner prep a breeze. Flip to the next page to see the three most common table configurations.

Everyday dinner:

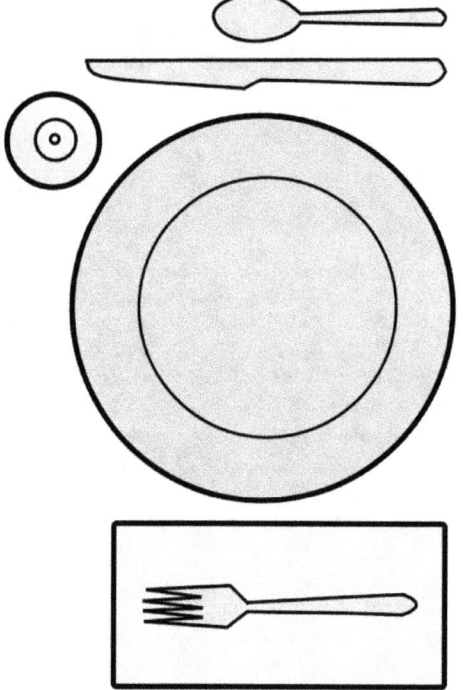

1. Lay out place mat (optional).
2. Place dinner plate in the centre.
3. Place fork on the left.
4. Place knife on the right, then place spoon right of knife.
5. Put water glass in top right, above the knife.
6. Place napkin on top of plate or beneath fork.

Casual meal:

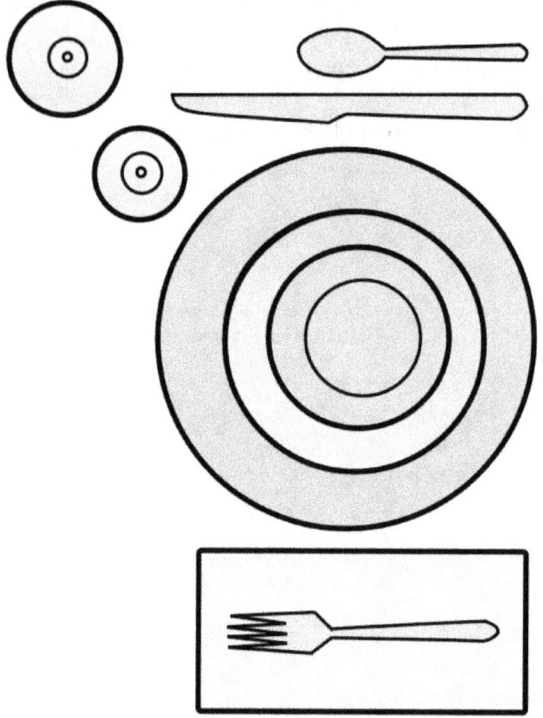

1. Lay out place mat (optional).

2. Place dinner plate in the centre.

3. Place salad plate on top of dinner plate (optional).

4. Place soup bowl on top of salad plate (optional).

5. Place knife to the right, then place spoon to the right of knife

6. Put water glass in top right, above the knife.

7. Put wineglass to the right of water glass.

8. Place napkin on top of plates or beneath fork.

Formal event:

1. Lay out tablecloth.
2. Place dinner plate in the centre.
3. Place salad plate on top of dinner plate.
4. Place bread plate above and left of plates, and rest butter knife horizontally across butter plate.
5. Place dinner fork on the left, then place salad fork to the left of dinner fork.
6. Place knife to the right, then place spoon to the right of knife.
7. Place dessert spoon horizontally above dinner plate.
8. Put water, white and red wineglasses in top right. Water glass should be closest, followed by white and red wine glasses.
9. Place napkin on top of salad plate.
10. Add place card above dessert spoon.
11. Place coffee cup and saucer below glasses with dessert plate.

Plate Language

As a guest, knowing basic plate language allows you to politely communicate to others your progress in the meal while avoiding awkwardness. Nothing worse than coming back from the bathroom to see your plate has vanished even though you're not done yet.

Plate language can get very fancy, and can even vary from country to country, but to avoid backfiring confusion and potential obnoxiousness, just stick to the basics.

Pause   Ready for second plate   Excellent

Finished   Do not like

Flower Language (basics)

What?! Just how many languages do I have to learn?! You might be laughing at how random this topic is. But you have to admit that flowers have had a strong connection to romance since the dawn of time. If your date is particularly interested in flowers, you can impress them with some basic knowledge of flower language.

Credit: Better Homes & Gardens

Some flowers that are particularly relevant to your love life include:

- ❖ Red roses, obviously
- ❖ Pink peonies
- ❖ White daisies
- ❖ Red tulips
- ❖ Purple asters

Each of those flowers symbolise romance, affection and passion. If you want to get fancier, however:

- ❖ Sunflowers are quirky and represent warmth and longevity. Good for anniversaries.
- ❖ Purple lilac represents early emotions of love.
- ❖ Daffodils are the tenth anniversary flower and represent devotion.
- ❖ Violets represent Sapphic desire, perfect for women that love women.

❖ Green carnations, popularised by Oscar Wilde, represent male same-sex romance.

The way you give these flowers to your date can also vary based on occasion. Of course, if it's a special event like an anniversary or birthday, have a nice big bouquet ready. If you want to surprise them with flowers somewhere, prepare it in a vase and wait until they discover it. And if you're more of the spontaneous romantic type, you can always just give them a single flower.

How to Sew a Button

It's the twenty-first century – every gender should know how to sew a button. You may ask, how is this related to romance? Well it's not, but it is an extremely useful skill. And as I said previously, knowing some basic skills that make you a functional human being is actually quite attractive. Plus, it's quite sweet if you're able to fix your partner's blouse or shirt. They'll appreciate it more than if they had got someone else to fix it or bought a new shirt.

1. Start by threading your needle and tying a knot at the end. Make a small stitch directly under the button and bring up through one of the holes

2. If your button only has two holes then it's super easy, just keep going between each. There are a lot of patterns you can do for a four-hole button but the cross is probably the most straight-forward. All you need to do is to go through diagonal holes and stitching at the bottom each time until secure.

3. When done, tie off a knot under the fabric and cut off the remaining thread.

How to Waltz

Nowadays, many of us meet people at clubs and bars. There's drinking and dancing involved, but mostly drinking. When it comes to the dancing ... well ... all I can say is that it's evolved a lot throughout time. Now, the most common way you'd dance with your date may be by throwing your ass in a circle on the dancefloor. If you think that's great, then that's good for you. But occasionally, you may find yourself in a situation where you just want to hold your partner close and slowly dance with them to soft music. Whether you're in your kitchen at 10p.m. or you're doing your first dance on your wedding night, it's good to know how to waltz.

As you know, here in *The Wingman's Handbook*, I'm all about inclusivity. Because of that, I'm eliminating gender roles and will be calling them A and B.

First of all, you need to know how to hold your partner. The waltz uses a common starting position called the Closed Position, where person A will have their left hand on person B's right shoulder, and their right hand is holding person B's left hand. B will hold A's right hand with their left hand and rest their right hand on A's waist.

The waltz is actually not that hard to do right, but it's also not that hard to mess up, hence why so many people are certain they can do it but end up looking super bad. As you may know, the waltz is written in ¾ time, which means that you count beats of three. Therefore, your steps will be in sync to that. The basic waltz steps are box steps, which mean all you have to do is make a box with your feet, to the beat of ¾. To visualise, I've also included some diagrams of what a waltz would look like for person A and B respectively.

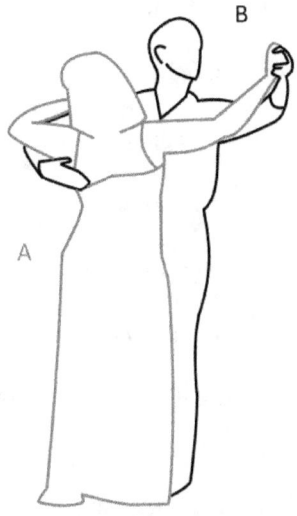

For Person A

Start with your feet in the 5-6 position.

1. Step back with right foot.
2. Step to the left with left foot.
3. Bring right foot next to left foot.
4. Step forward with left foot.
5. Step forward sideways with right foot.
6. Bring left foot next to right foot.

For Person B

Start with your feet in the 5-6 position.

1. Step forward with left foot.

2. Step to the right with right foot.

3. Bring left foot next to right foot.

4. Step forward with right foot.

5. Step forward sideways with left foot.

6. Bring right foot next to left foot.

So, those are the bare basics of the waltz. If you're ready to spice it up, here are two things you can do:

1. **Add some direction –** The ballroom is usually pretty big, so what's the point of cramping you and your partner up in the same place, drawing the same square over and over? If you are Person B, you can lead the direction of the waltz with Person A. To do so, next time you take a step forward, instead of stepping directly forward, angle your step out. Follow suit with your left hand, which should be holding Person A's right hand. The angle and size of the stride you take will determine the direction you are heading, and how you rotate your extended left hand will change your angle. Here's what your footwork may look like after you add in some natural turns.

2. **Do a spin (aka Underarm turn)** - Occasionally sprinkling in a spin looks pretty fancy, and it's also fun to do. To do it, first Person A continues the first half of the box normally. Once A has stepped backwards, then sideways, then closed the box, B will release their right hand and raise their left hand (which is holding A's right hand). A can then pivot on their right hand to the right for around three steps. Then, B should be rotating to their right ready to meet A again in the closed position. Sounds complicated, but really isn't.

With these basic moves, it should be good enough for most occasions. Of course, you can always learn more complexities for dancing, but this is the basic skillset for those that just don't want to embarrass themselves in front of their crush.

How to Take Good Photos

Have you ever gone out with someone, asked them to take a few photos of you, because your outfit was especially popping that day, but then the photos turn out to be shit because your friend kept shaking? Or maybe you were the one that was tasked to be a photographer and you just didn't give a shit? Well, no matter which of those people you are, and how little you care about photos, it's still good to know how to take good photos.

Here are some concepts that make for a photograph:

Composition - Composition in a photo refers to the shapes, textures and colours that make up a photo. It's easy to capture an object or setting in a photo, but what makes it truly pleasant to look at is how everything is arranged. One composition trick that works quite well is the rule of thirds. This principle refers to balancing your image with a 3x3 grid. By placing your subject in any third, it will give your picture satisfying symmetry or quirky asymmetry.

Here are a few examples of the rule of thirds being used. In both of these images, we see the use of symmetrical thirds and asymmetrical thirds.

Angle – Taking photos can be much more interesting than just snapping your subject at eye-level. You can reserve that for passports, driver's licences and mugshots. Tilting up or down can create completely different effects and even alter the appearance of your subject.

For example, shooting from a higher angle makes your subject look small, which can give off a harmless and cute vibe. From that angle, it also sharpens their face, making it appear slimmer.

With a low angle, your subject will be given a sense of empowerment. This angle also interestingly elongates them, giving them a more slender appearance. This is especially nice for people that want to show off their legs. Be mindful to not actually get so low you see up their nose, or that's just weird.

Framing – Similar to composition, but the exact opposite. Instead of focusing on how you arrange the subject to fit in a photo, framing is how you arrange the camera to fit the subject. The amount of space you put into the photo influences the relationship of the subject's position to the viewer.

A photo where the person takes up most of frame (so a close-up) focuses on the emotions of the subject. The closeness also makes it feel more intimate, and in some cases, claustrophobic.

On the other hand, framing the subject from afar creates a lot of what we call 'white space', which are portions of the photo that aren't the main focus. This type of framing is used to focus on a person's physical relationship to their surroundings.

Line of sight – Science shows us that people's eyes like to track paths in things they see as opposed to randomly scanning. For those that have had to say to people 'hey, my eyes are up here', you probably get it. In photography, lines that run along an image to direct the eyes of a viewer are called 'leading lines'. They can add motion and depth to a picture.

Other random tips to finish off with:

- ❖ Candid shots (or at least staged candid) look good. You don't always need to make your subject freeze in front of the camera with a big smile plastered on.

❖ Make use of props you have. Maybe you and your date happen to be out while raining, well, now that umbrella is a great prop for your photoshoot.

- ❖ Taking a photo from behind is an interesting way of incorporating the scenery. Put something interesting in their line of sight and your photo tells a story

❖ For those that want to look like they have slim legs, when you take a photo of them, be sure to include a little bit of thigh to outline the leg's width

People and Relationships

It's no surprise that how you deal with other people is especially important when it comes to relationships. So in this final category of guides, I'm going to run you through a few techniques that will improve your way with words. Oh, and I also threw in a tutorial on how to kiss, cause your mouth isn't just used for talking.

The Art of Assertiveness

Assertiveness, essentially, is one type of communication style. The other styles you may have heard of include passive, aggressive and passive aggressive. You can tell what style a person uses based on visible cues like body language, tone of voice and whatnot, but the core determinant is how they balance their own needs with others.

First up, here's an overview of the four communication styles:

Passive

- ❖ Low self-esteem
- ❖ Submissive
- ❖ Needs Approval
- ❖ Denial
- ❖ Shame
- ❖ Weak boundaries
- ❖ Self-inhibiting

- ❖ Apologetic
- ❖ Shy

Aggressive

- ❖ Explosive
- ❖ Violent
- ❖ Dominant
- ❖ Power-hungry
- ❖ Threatening
- ❖ Hostile
- ❖ Overbearing
- ❖ Egoistic
- ❖ Intolerant

Passive-aggressive

- ❖ Manipulative
- ❖ Indirect
- ❖ Dishonest
- ❖ Resentful
- ❖ Vengeful
- ❖ Sarcastic

- ❖ Backhanded
- ❖ Stubborn
- ❖ Apathetic

Assertive

- ❖ Honest
- ❖ Empathetic
- ❖ Confident
- ❖ Expressive
- ❖ Direct
- ❖ Accepting
- ❖ Firm
- ❖ Active
- ❖ Comfortable

Now, let's take a closer at each of them and how you can identify which is your own communication style.

Passive

The communication style where a person sacrifices their own needs for others'.

Behaviour – passive people are usually shy and have low self-esteem. They may constantly seek approval of others. This makes them highly vulnerable to being 'walked over'. In appearance, passive people frequently exhibit low-confidence body language, such as little eye contact, slumped body posture and nervousness.

Conflict – passive people will most likely avoid confrontation if possible. They do this by not expressing their thoughts and feelings if they will cause any type of dispute. If directly confronting conflict, they will become apologetic and yield to others.

Consequences – because passive people will often let others infringe on their rights, many feel helpless and depressed. They may also feel resentful that their needs are neglected but do nothing about it. Passive people may also feel confused and be unable to understand their own feelings as they are frequently repressed.

Examples

"It's okay; you can do whatever you want."

"I'm afraid of speaking up."

"I want to make everyone happy."

"I don't know."

Aggressive

The complete opposite of passive, an aggressive communication style refers to someone that will sacrifice everyone else's needs for their own.

Behaviour – Aggressive people are unyielding and don't care for other people, and will use verbal or physical force to get what they want. They demonstrate hostile behaviour. Contrary to popular belief, aggressive people also have low self-esteem and negatively associate abuse to healthy communication.

Conflict – As aggressive people care little about other's needs, they will frequently incite conflict with their way of expressing thoughts and opinions. When conflict arises, they will use humiliation, criticism and blame to attack others. Aggressive people are also overbearing, and desire to control others. They are interrupting, threatening and impulsive.

Consequences – The aggression of these people will usually lead to their alienation. Those around aggressive people typically feel fear and hatred. Aggressive people constantly blame others for their own problems, therefore will fail to deal with problems maturely.

Examples

"Because I said so!"

"Everything is your fault."

"I feel I am always right."

"I always get what I want."

Passive Aggressive

First observed in WWII, passive-aggressive communicators use indirectness and subtlety to meet their needs while appearing cooperative and submissive.

Behaviour - Passive aggressive people often feel resentful and powerless. They lack courage to directly deal with issues. Their body language can be deceiving, since they will appear compliant and friendly, but feel distasteful inside. Passive-aggressive people are vengeful and sarcastic.

Conflict - Passive-aggressive people avoid direct conflict, and instead will express their anger indirectly. Using manipulation, passive-aggressive people can covertly use others to their advantage. They also use backhanded compliments, sabotage and the silent treatment to deal out emotional damage to others.

Consequences - Passive aggressive people can become alienated by others due to the discomfort and hurt they cause to others. This communication style will get them nowhere, and they will remain powerless. While they express resentment, it is unproductive as they will never directly address the issue.

Examples

"I mean, you can if you want, it's your choice."

"Oh well, whatever."

"I'm not mad."

"I was only joking, calm down."

Assertive

And finally, assertiveness. Assertive communicators clearly ensure their needs are met, but also won't sacrifice other's needs.

Behaviour – Assertive people are confident and value their thoughts and opinions. However, they're also empathetic and understand other people's needs and wants. They exhibit confident body language with good eye contact and a relaxed posture. Assertive people feel in control of their own feelings and are great communicators.

Conflict – When faced with conflict, an assertive person strongly resists abuse and manipulation used against them. They will advocate strongly, but respectfully, for themselves to avoid causing unnecessary harm. They will attempt to solve a problem the fairest way possible to ensure everyone's needs are met.

Consequences – Assertive people feel a deep connection to others due to their ability to communicate well. They are also in control of their lives and can maturely address problems directly. They provide a positive influence on others to be fair and mature themselves.

Examples

"We are both equally entitled to express our opinions."

"No one tells me how to feel except myself."

"Can you tell me how you feel?"

"I don't think this is fair for me."

Assertiveness is the best form of communication. As it creates a balance between your needs and other people's needs, you'll become someone who can get what you deserve fairly, but also be a pleasant and considerate person for others. So, how can you start becoming more assertive?

1. **Be honest and open** – Convey your thoughts openly to others and encourage them to do the same.

2. **Set boundaries** – Know your personal limits and enforce them without being a bully.

3. **Be an active listener** – Listen to others with your heart and don't interrupt.

4. **Take perspective** – Understand that two opinions can both be right while being different.

5. **Don't guilt trip** – Avoid becoming passive aggressive by being honest about your feelings to others.

6. **Stay calm** – Use relaxed body language and don't show hostility.

7. **Be a problem-solver** – Direct your focus on dealing with the problem, not the person.

8. **Use assertive body language** – Stay friendly but firm when delivering your message.

9. **Learn to say no** – Avoid being walked over and let others know civilly if your rights are being violated.

10. **Be patient** – Understand that switching to an assertive style isn't instantaneous and will take practice.

Luckily, we aren't stuck with the communication style we are born with. Assertiveness can be developed. Next up, we're going to learn how to start being assertive in the way we talk. Welcome to the 'build-an-assertive-phrase' workshop!

Assertive communicators frequently use 'I' statements, such as 'I think' and 'I feel'. These are excellent because they are probably the most direct phrases you can use to convey your feelings.

Also, here's a good template for assertive sentences that enable you to explain your response to someone.

When you [situation], it makes me feel [emotion] because [reason].

This sentence template is the Holy Grail, because it can be used in any context. It provides a straightforward expression of your thoughts to someone.

Let's say you come home from work exhausted and are dismayed to see that the dishes you told your partner so many times to wash are still sitting there in the sink. After getting over your emotions, you need to talk to them about this. Using the template, you might say something like this:

"When you leave the dishes in the sink after I ask you to clean them, it makes me feel disrespected because it's like you haven't taken my words seriously."

Now, how would this interaction go for the other communication styles?

Passive: (Say nothing about it and wash dishes)

Aggressive: "Are you stupid or something? I've told you to wash the dishes so many fucking times!"

Passive-aggressive: "Wow, look at all these dishes. Nothing better than coming home to a dirty sink."

Reading all the other options, it's obvious that the assertive communication style is the best. It's straightforward and honest but isn't rude. Your needs are also conveyed without compromising. Because you're being specific with both situation and emotion, it can help your partner to make things better. As you already know, problems in a relationship can only be fixed if the two people can communicate to each other what's wrong and how it affects you both.

How to Console a Partner

Nothing breaks my heart more than seeing a partner upset about anything. I feel myself in their exact situation, and I'm like 100% sure that I'll cry too when they start tearing up. Does that sound like you? If you're an empath, you'll understand this very well.

But interestingly enough, many people struggle to console their partners despite knowing exactly how they feel. That's because empathy doesn't immediately grant you the skill of consoling. If you're a natural at this, feel free to skip this guide. However, if you're like me and die on the inside with heartbreak but get super awkward about it, then this is for you.

1. **Talk about it** – If you can tell they're upset, but they haven't initiated a conversation with you yet, let them know that they can talk to you about it when they feel comfortable to. If they've already started talking to you, then engage them in conversation. Talking about something with a person you love really does wonders.

2. **Never be judgemental** – We're all people with different opinions and personalities. Even your partner isn't going to be your perfect fit. Just for this moment, throw away your judgements and listen to your partner. What you feel is stupid or insignificant might actually be a big deal for them. Belittling your partner's problems is a sure-fire way to make the matter worse.

3. **Don't make assumptions** – Never try to read your partner's mind. No matter how well you know them, you just can't. So, if they refuse to talk to you for the time being, don't immediately jump to conclusions that it's your fault or they don't trust you. In a way, accusing them of those things really projects your inner fears and insecurities.

4. **Give space** – While you encourage them to talk to you, also give them space when they need it. Be able to read signs that they're feeling overwhelmed or pressured. Not everyone is immediately ready to talk about something that has just happened. Sometimes giving your partner space to sort their feelings out is the greatest act of care you can give them.

5. **Be there** – It's good to remind your partner that you'll be there whenever they need, and that you've got their best interests at heart. And then when a crisis happens, *actually* be there. People who are neglected at their lowest times suffer immense emotional damage. Don't be that person.

Consoling by Love Language
While the above points will help you be in the right attitude to console your partner, it's important to also remember that everyone feels comfort differently. Using love languages, you can enhance the effectiveness of your consoling.

Words of affirmation – Obviously, if your partner values words, then they'll really appreciate talking to you. Encourage them to tell you everything when they're comfortable, and listen to them with your heart. Reminding them verbally that you're always there for them, no matter what, will help.

Effective consolation phrases that don't sound fake:

- ❖ "I care about you"
- ❖ "You matter to me"
- ❖ "You make total sense to me"
- ❖ "What can I do to help?"

Physical touch – Have you ever heard people talk about the power of touch? We are social mammals, so contact is definitely something that many of us enjoy. In fact, there have been studies that show cuddling up with people we love can greatly increase our oxytocin levels. So, if your partner values touch they'll definitely value:

- ❖ A hug, obviously.
- ❖ A kiss (on the forehead is usually best for these types of situations).
- ❖ Prolonged cuddling. Whatever you're doing, it's probably just nice to hold them for a bit.
- ❖ Idle touching when talking. Maybe stroking their hair, running fingertips up and down their arm or back.
- ❖ A reaffirming hand on their shoulder or squeeze of the hand.

Quality time – In this busy world, how often can we slow down to really listen to what others have to say? Sometimes, just your presence is enough to make your partner feel better. If that sounds like your partner, here are some other actions to do for this love language:

- ❖ Dedicate your time to listening to their feelings and listen with your heart.
- ❖ Take your partner out somewhere they like to blow off some steam.
- ❖ Watch a funny movie together for a temporary distraction.
- ❖ If you can't see them in person, call or FaceTime them.

Acts of service - If your partner's love language is acts of service, they'll appreciate your actions in consoling them. Instead of saying 'it gets better', show them that it really does get better with these things:

- ❖ Give them the day to heal by doing all the chores and boring stuff.
- ❖ Offer to draw a bath, or anything else you know that will relax them.
- ❖ Sit them down and work together on a solution.
- ❖ Actively ask them what you can do to make them feel better.

Receiving gifts – This love language is quite challenging to do when put in the context of consoling. However, there are people that prefer material demonstrations of love, so if that's your partner, you can try these things:

- ❖ Give them a sympathy/cheer-up card.

- ❖ Get them a little memento that will remind them you're always there for them.

- ❖ If they require a particular thing to solve their problem, get them the thing.

- ❖ Give them a box of little hand-written notes from you to remind them of your support.

As you've have learnt, people can speak more than one love language and sometimes one language more than the other at any given time. You may try one thing that worked in one context but not in another, so be mindful of that. Once you know your partner very well, you'll find it easier and easier to console them, not just because you understand what works, but because your heart is in tune to theirs.

Saying No

There are many reasons why someone might struggle with this particular word. They may have come from an overbearing background where they had little power, experienced negative events where they felt helpless, or are just too kind as a person. Whatever the reason, learning how to say 'no' is super, super important because this two-letter word holds a tremendous amount of power in any context and any relationship.

It can be especially challenging when you have to say 'no' to your partner. That's because we're always expected to be completely on the same page as them, unconditionally. And we're afraid that, by saying 'no', we are demonstrating a lack of love. But that's not the case. Your partner isn't a mind reader, they'll never be 100% sure what will satisfy you or not. In fact, if you can say no, your partner will appreciate it because they can learn more about your limits, likes, and dislikes.

On a larger scope, society has coded the word to be uncaring and selfish, especially for women, and while it may be true sometimes, we've developed such a strong reaction to it that we avoid the word, even if it violates our own beliefs. Remember the communication styles we talked about earlier? Passive people will find saying 'no' the hardest, because they lack the integrity to hold themselves up. Research even shows us that the inability to say 'no' is linked with low self-confidence.

No is a complete sentence – That's a cliché phrase, but it has a lot of depth. Except for certain situations, you don't owe people an apology with your 'no'. You don't need to write a 1,000-word essay to justify your use of the word. You don't need to add a 'but' and then a condition to satisfy the other person's ego to your expense. You can just say no. And remember that. If you don't put your foot down, no one else will do it for you.

So, here's how you can start saying 'no' comfortably and not be afraid of the word:

1. **Keep it simple** – Remember, it's a complete sentence. Spare the wishy-washy stuff if you want your sentence to be delivered and understood. Keep it firm and direct. Use assertive body language to stand your ground. If you're muttering 'no' and looking like a breeze will knock you over, then guess what? The other person will see that and coerce you into saying 'yes'.

2. **Take some time** – If you're someone that always defaults to 'yes', then immediately answering 'no' to someone can be quite hard. It's okay to give yourself some time to mull over your response, and to gather some confidence. There's no shame in that, just respond to the person with "I'll get back to you".

3. **Think of a compromise** – While I talked about avoiding 'but', sometimes it can be used to maintain a relationship you are afraid of damaging when saying 'no'. However, you need to do this strategically so it works out without you being walked over. Mind you, don't think of compromising if you

genuinely want or need to say no. Don't do this for life and death situations.

4. **Remember refusal ≠ rejection** – Many people are afraid of saying 'no' because it could hurt the other person's feelings. But it's important for us to remember that refusing someone doesn't mean you've socially rejected them. You need to separate the favour from the person.

5. **Be honest with yourself** – As said previously, don't let yourself be walked over. Know what you truly feel, your gut doesn't lie. Making yourself say 'yes' to something when your entire mind is feeling 'no' won't do anything except make you feel bad.

The good thing about saying 'no' is that you get better with practice. While it may seem difficult to rewire your brain away from defaulting to 'yes', it's possible with time and determination. Remember, learning to say 'no' does not make you a bad person; it doesn't make you an unkind person. In fact, when you think you're being kind to everyone by saying 'yes' to everything they ask, you're still an unkind person. That's because you're being unkind to yourself!

How to be a Good Listener

"People talking without speaking,

People hearing without listening"

Those are lyrics to 'The Sound of Silence' by Simon & Garfunkel. That just sounds like a weirdly poetic quote, but these two lines really pack a lot of meaning. Being a good listener is more than just receiving the sound waves of someone's voice with your ear. No, that's called hearing, and most of the population can do that. To be a good listener, you don't just use your ears, but also your heart.

Characteristics of a Good Listener

Here are some characteristics you might have brainstormed:

- ❖ Maintaining eye contact.
- ❖ Not interrupting.
- ❖ Displaying interest by nodding and smiling at appropriate times.
- ❖ Asking follow-up questions to engage speaker.
- ❖ Not changing subject.

These are all valid points. They all revolve around your ability to explicitly display interest and respect to the speaker. Being a good listener is an extremely valuable trait as a romantic partner because your partner's going to be sharing a lot with you. When you're emotionally intimate with someone, you'll feel compelled to talk to them about everything. Knowing that you're being listened to makes you feel respected and loved, and that's exactly the type of feeling you're trying to give your partner and get from your partner as well.

It's surprisingly easy to be a bad listener. Maybe we're too occupied with our own problems, or lack the ability to tap into someone's feelings, or we are simply too caught up in our own busy lives. When your partner comes home from a long day of work and tries to tell you what's upsetting you, you'll hear their voice, but not listen to a single thing they say. And guess what? Most people can tell the difference when someone is listening to them or not. No matter whether your partner reacts by angrily reminding you that they're speaking, or just slowly trail off, this'll hurt them for a while.

This topic is a good follow-up to the previous tutorial on how to be good at consoling. However, being a good listener is more than just lending your ear and heart to your partner when they tell you what's hurting them. And in this section, you'll see that I'm actually trying to teach you something else.

The Four Styles of Responding to Good News

In relationships, we make an unspoken promise that we'll be there for each other when things get rough. 'Will you be there when things go wrong?' And so, most of us are. And through resilience, love and determination, we overcome relationship hurdles together. But what I want to know now is, 'will you be there when things go right?' When we talk about good listening, we always tend to think of it in a consoling, therapeutic way. But good listening is equally - if not more - important for sharing good news.

Dr Shelly Gable is a psychologist from California, and she researched the ways couples responded to good news. She then came up with the four main ways of response.

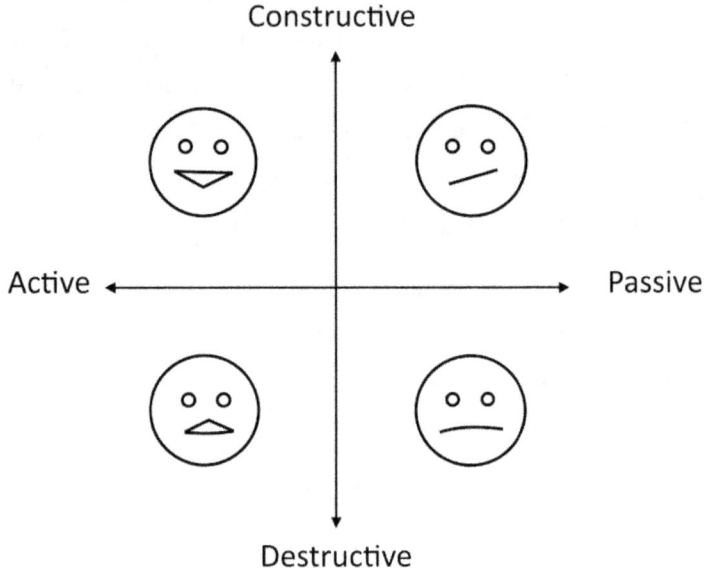

The four styles are separated with two sets of descriptors:

Active – Being directly engaged in a conversation.

Passive – Not directly engaged in conversation.

Constructive – Supportive behaviour for speaker.

Destructive – Unsupportive behaviour for speaker.

Out of the four styles, there's only one that can contribute to the growth and improvement of an intimate relationship. The other three will create distance and negative feelings. And of course, you've probably figured it out by now, but the effective style is <u>Active Constructive Responding</u> (ACR).

Let's break down the chart. When we're looking at Passive Constructive responses, they're supportive, but very low energy. To the speaker, it can feel pretty insincere. The unresponsiveness can also pretty much guarantee that the conversation will just die on the spot. If done via online messaging, we call this <u>dry texting</u>, and everyone hates that. On the other side of the passive axes is Passive Destructive. Now here, the unresponsiveness and disinterest still show, but the listener usually then goes forward and straight up changes the subject, either to talk about themselves (self-deprecating or self-inflating), or just any other random topic. Now, that's really disrespectful and a sure-fire way to kill any enthusiasm and happiness the speaker would have. Both passive responses are classified by a general disinterest in the good news that is being delivered. People that exhibit passive response styles will usually fail to maintain eye contact with the speaker, are distracted by other things and angle away from the speaker.

Alright, so now the Active responses. Active Destructive responses mean exactly what you think they mean. When listening to the speaker, they will engage with the topic, but may exhibit criticising or dismissive behaviour. This means they'll immediately express criticism or identify flaws in the good news that they've just heard. Alternatively, they may also discredit the speaker by showing genuine disbelief (as in actually thinking they're bullshit, not the excited half-assed 'I can't believe it!'). By doing this stuff, the speaker's excited mood can quickly change into either anxiety, since they're starting to question themselves if the good news was actually good; or anger, because they feel like they're being insulted. You can pretty much imagine what this response style is going to do to a speaker. You've literally just ripped the lollipop out of their hands, and chucked it in the bin. It's no surprise Active Destructive completely wrecks relationships.

And of course, now we come down to Active Constructive Responding. Active responders, especially ACR, all exhibit body language of engagement – eye contact, angling towards the speaker, leaning away from distractions and direct responses to the topic. However, ACR means showing authentic and visible engagement to the speaker. When you congratulate them, you really mean it. Someone demonstrating ACR will show more positive emotions and body language. When you really do feel intensely happy for your partner, you'll see yourself closing the distance between you and your partner. Maybe you'll show wide-eyed disbelief (but not too much of course). Maybe you might find yourself subconsciously squeezing their hand, wondering how you manage to meet someone as brilliant as them.

After reading all of these responsive styles, you might have identified which response style you use with your partner (because people can have different response styles to different people). Remember, the key here is to do ACR, because that's the only one that will improve a relationship's trust and intimacy. The truth is that many of us don't do the bad styles on purpose. If we all knew what styles were harmful, we'd immediately stop. There are many factors that can contribute to us failing to do ACR, like stress, fatigue, a bad habit of derailing conversations and pessimism. Luckily, it's possible for us to unlearn any of the other styles and adopt ACR.

How? Well first of all, you need some gratitude to appreciate that someone is sharing their good news with you. If you're able to feel grateful about something like that, it'll discourage you from feeling uninterested in them or wanting to change the subject.

Next, you need to ask yourself this question: What does it mean for you to be authentically engaged? The reality is that ACR isn't the same formula for everyone. Everyone displays <u>authentic engagement</u> differently, but the main connecting point is everyone has a method at least. So, think back to the last time you've felt genuinely happy for someone's good news (and believe me, no matter how much you practise the other styles, there's ought to be at least one time you recall where you feel you were authentically engaged), and answer the question.

What does it mean for you to be authentically engaged? Do you:

- ❖ Ask follow-up questions?

- ❖ Show interested body language?
- ❖ Drop whatever you're doing to listen?
- ❖ Suggest celebration activities afterwards?
- ❖ Increase your demonstration of positive emotions like excitement?

Once you find out, you'll find that doing ACR with your partner will be a breeze, and in turn, you'll see your relationship grow drastically.

How to Kiss (Well)

Ah, kissing. Such a joy. We as humans have been kissing for a very long time. And when I say a long time, I mean thousands of years. It's a way of social bonding I guess. And as the mouth is an erogenous zone, it feels good. Can confirm.

Even though the act of kissing is so familiar to humanity, it can feel unfamiliar at the same time. Sure, it seems pretty straightforward; you just press your lips on someone else's lips. But what makes it so much more daunting when it comes to kissing in a romantic context? Well, you can blame society for that, as you can with almost every other problem I've explored in this book. There's a certain social pressure put on us to be able to kiss well. And a lot of us can feel pretty disappointed if we don't nail it the first time, but guess what? Just like riding a bike, no one does it perfect first time. And also like riding a bike, the only way you can get better at it is to do it more. So, to all my relationship rookies out there in their first relationship, here's your 100% valid excuse to smooch with your partner more!

First Kiss
Alright, so to begin, I'm going to prep you for your first kiss.

1. **GET CONSENT!** This is really important, especially if it's also their first kiss too! Consent isn't just something that goes for sex - it goes for any sort of intimate contact, including hugs and kisses. Of course, verbal consent often isn't something you'll see later on in your relationships, but when you're this early on, you probably don't know your partner

well enough yet to be able to read their body cues so it's best to be safe by asking if you can kiss them. Also, don't you think it's kinda cute to do that? Well I know I do.

2. **Throw out your expectations** – It's not going to be 100% perfect and dreamlike. Oh and fun fact, your first kiss doesn't necessarily have to be a long dramatic make-out session, in the way movies show it. Mine definitely wasn't, it was just a peck on the lips. In your first few attempts at kissing, things will most likely get in the way. Stuff like your hair, teeth and nose. Don't feel discouraged though, it happens to everybody.

3. **Relax** – Man, I can't stress this enough. In day-to-day life, we all hold a lot of subconscious tension. Right now, unclench your jaw, loosen your shoulders and take a deep breath. This new relaxed state you're in right now should be the state you should be in when you go in for your first kiss. It's understandable to be nervous, but too much tension ruins performance.

4. **Make your lips kissable** – At least keep them nice and moisturised. I'm speaking from personal observations around me, avoid those fancy sweet flavoured chapsticks at all cost. They are absolute shit and do nothing but dry your lips out more. That's a capitalist trick to make you buy more. Aim for the more boring-looking, plain-tasting ones with long chemical names on the box. These ones usually contain extra stuff in them that actually help hydrate your lips.

5. **Choose a good setting** - Tying in with the first point on consent, it is never okay to ask your partner for a first kiss in a setting where they will feel pressured to do so. What's an example of a bad setting? Let's think of a frat party where all your friends are chanting at both of you "Kiss them! Kiss them!" If your partner's totally fine with a situation like that, then go for it. Remember, it's all about the consent. It's not a prerequisite for the setting of your first kiss to be a super isolated, super romantic place. Not all of us have instant access to a private Jacuzzi, unfortunately. However, it's still good to respect the wishes of your partner and find an appropriate opportunity to do it.

Kissing and the Senses

Alright, so we're all prepped. Now for the real stuff. This can be applied to not just the first kiss, but for any other kisses in the future too!

We have to understand that the act of kissing well (the keyword being well) relies on many forces to act at once. Unless you're very observant when watching movies or other people kiss, we can be so focused on looking at the mouths that we fail to notice all the other things going on. So, what are the components of a good kiss? To be able to engage all of the senses, or most of them anyways. If you've noticed, we normally kiss with the eyes closed. Opening your eyes while you kiss can be seen as insincere. Why? Well just like how most people like to have sex with the lights off, depriving ourselves of the sense of sight greatly boosts our experience of the other senses. Sight is probably the most overwhelming sense of them all in day-to-day life.

So, how are each of the senses engaged during a kissing session?

Sight - Before you actually kiss, you can briefly lock eye contact with your partner. This helps you see where you're going (closing your eyes too early is awkward), and also creates a lot of intimacy. Eye contact is a form of emotional connection after all. When you actually go in, close your eyes.

Hearing - Not a very dominant sense, but can be used to gauge their breathing, as well as your own breathing. For some people, hearing their breathing can be kind of hot I guess. On the topic of breathing, be sure to breath from your nose often or you'll run out of breath. Too many times have I made this rookie mistake in my early days and had to pull out and take large gulps of air. It's not flattering at all.

Smell - Did you know that humans actually remember people more fondly by their scent than what they look like? Help intensify the make out session by wearing a nice perfume or cologne. At the same time, since you're getting so close to your partner, you'll be able to notice their scent. While we're talking about noses, avoid bumping noses by tilting your head to the opposite side of your partner. This isn't something you plan prior, but everyone usually favours a side, and you'll discover how your partner leans through repeated experience.

Taste - If they're wearing flavoured lipstick or chapstick, you'll definitely taste it, but only very faintly. On the flip side, if your partner has bad breath, you'll notice it. It's good practice for you and your partner to keep breath mints or gum on yourself. It's one part of the Romance Kit which I put together in part 10. When your lips actually come together, they won't be pressed together symmetrically. Because your heads will be slightly tilted and your lips will be slightly open, the effect you're going for is essentially lip stacking. Just like head tilting, you'll figure out who takes the top lip through practical experience.

Touch – If you choose to use tongue, it's gonna be touching a lot of places. Please don't wave it around like a snake, that's going to terrify your partner. Instead, to ask your partner nonverbally to French, start off by brushing your tongue lightly on their lips. If they break off, that's an obvious no. If they let you in, start easy. One trick you can try is to trace the alphabet in their mouth. Also, your hands shouldn't be stiff by your side. Use them! Whether you're going to cup their cheeks or full-on caress them everywhere, it's nice extra sensory stimulation.

It may seem daunting after reading that. How am I going to be able to remember all of these processes when I kiss? Well the good news is you'll find yourself doing most of these naturally. Through practice you can fully master all your senses and give the best experience to yourself and your partner.

Part 10

Earning Your Wings

And here we are, in the final chapter of the book. It surely has been a ride. I've never met you in person, but I feel like I've been there with you for a long time, and I plan to be there when you go on your first date and when you're healing yourself after a break-up.

As you go through life, you'll find romance happening not only to you, but to others around you. Perhaps you want to be able to help your friends with their love lives, because you understand dating sucks in this economy. Assuming that you've read the entire book already, I'll deem you qualified enough to be able to read on and gain access to all a wingman's tools of the trade. If you just got this book and skipped to this chapter, I highly recommend that you go all the way back to part 1.

The Art of Third Wheeling

Before we begin, I'm gonna take it back a step. Let's first talk about pop cultures' most pitiful role - the third wheel. A third wheel is the title given to anyone that plays a particularly redundant and awkward role in a social outing that sees the other two people interacting, leaving the third wheel out. It doesn't even have to be the third person following after a couple. Third wheels can appear even in regular friendship groups, which probably hurts more because we perceive friendships as all equal to each other, like an interconnected net. But unfortunately, that's not always the case.

So why am I talking about this before I teach you how to be a wingman? That's because both of these roles require you to be a person who is *outside* of someone's relationship, but still be involved. More often than not, a person might simultaneously be a wingman and a third wheel. Because I didn't get into relationships at the same time as my friends did in school, there were many instances where I would be wingmanning while single. So, learning to be a good third wheel is a precursor for being a successful wingman. Although many people despise being a third wheel and respond with bitterness to their coupled-up friends (which is then met with more bitterness), that's not a productive mindset. We have to be smart and resourceful about things in our life to succeed. Remember the things I talked about earlier in my story – when we can't control the situation, we control our mind.

Alright, so if you find yourself becoming a third wheel, first convince yourself that it isn't a bad thing at all. Yep, that's right. There are many good benefits to third wheeling.

1. You've got two friends, more is always better.
2. There's no need to share food, like couples do.
3. If they invite you to their vacation then guess what? Free trips!
4. You've got access to both people's POV.

5. Now you have access to two new circles of friends.

6. You have two people to look out for you.

7. You'll get plenty of wingman practice as both people will consult you for help.

8. You can learn real practical information on maintaining a relationship.

9. You'll learn to adjust to single life, which means future break-ups won't hit you that hard.

10. Your friends can remind you that love exists out there, even for you.

See? It's not that bad. The only person making you feel resentful about your third wheel status is yourself. If your friends are good, they'll totally understand your third wheel status and try to make it as bearable as they can for you. Additionally, they'll really appreciate having a close friend that isn't their partner. That's because if they relied on their partner for all of their support and disaster strikes between them, they will have no one to help them.

Let's take a look at some etiquette of being a good third wheel. A good third wheel is one that is totally supportive of the relationship, feels comfortable and isn't in the way. A bad third wheel is one that is bitter, a drag to be with and generally unhelpful. You wouldn't want to be the second one because, trust me, it's very tiring for the couple, who is already trying to be nice by including you on their outings.

Alright, so how to be a good third wheel.

1. **Be normal** – Look, being a third wheel isn't *that* impactful on your life. It's a role you'll have for a while maybe, but your whole life isn't going to revolve around it. Just take it easy and continue your life as usual. Take your mind off your third wheel status and distract yourself with your normal life.

2. **Be smart** – Long-term third wheels develop really good social awareness due to their long-term exposure to couples. When you third wheel, you're most likely not going to be the most emotionally-connected person out of the three. That's a shame but you'll just have to work with what you have. With social awareness, you can tell when the couple has had a bit of a fight and probably doesn't want you bringing up their relationship. Or, they may be looking for an opportunity to do some 'couple things' and want to be left alone. You see, people rarely directly communicate thoughts like those because they don't want to be come off as rude. So you need to be smart and read these things.

3. **Be productive** – Make the most of your time as a third wheel! With two of your good friends in a relationship, you can always consult them if you want advice on finding love. At the same time, when you're at an outing, immerse yourself in the event so you have fun, and be supportive of your friends. Actively withdrawing yourself from the outing as a form of protest is going to help no one, and just make them not want to invite you to things in the future. Alternatively, don't invade their private space too much. Winking at them and

making too many sexual jokes will also make you annoying as hell. As said in the above point, be smart and don't embarrass yourself or your friends.

4. **Be positive** – Stop telling yourself that your third wheel status is a life sentence. Chances are it won't be. While you third wheel your friends, keep a look out for your own love life. If you choose to feel bitter about being trapped in a third wheel status, you've got no one else to blame but yourself. Your friends didn't force you to be a third wheel. So have a positive attitude.

Now that you are mentally sorted with being a third wheel, let's delve into the technical stuff of being a wingman, which includes a lot more knowledge and involvement.

Traits of a Good Wingman

Everyone can be well-informed about romance, but not everyone finds they're effective wingmen. That's because wingmen need to be able to devote themselves to the cause, even if it may compromise their own love life. The role of the wingman is a serving one, after all. So, what makes you a wingman, rather than just someone that has experience in romance?

Observation - Finding love, dating, flirting. All of these processes require the ability to read social cues and atmosphere of a situation. Wingmen are human surveillance cameras. By reading the slightest movements of someone at the club, or by sensing the sudden shift in tone of a party, they can gather information and effectively relay it to their buddy.

Perspective - The ability to take multiple viewpoints at once is highly valuable. This makes a wingman flexible and free from bias, which is greatly needed for solving problems. To have perspective can mean that a wingman might even have to give up personal views for true neutrality.

Problem solving - Hear me out, but problems between two people are never fixable with a text-book. I guess that's the beauty of the unpredictability of humans. However, as a wingman, you'll understand that no two cases are ever the same. Using both the juices of creativity and critical thinking, wingmen can create the best solution for any situation.

Honesty – Well, when you're trusted with giving advice, you can't hold back. A wingman is able to give an honest opinion, even if it's not nice, to ensure the best for their buddy. At the same time, a wingman will also be able to endure the backlash they may receive for honest opinions, because we all know how clouded some people can be when they're in love.

Investigative – To wingmen, the world is their playground and they can find any information they want with their seemingly infinite resources. Upon learning of new people, relationships or situations, wingmen will be quick to find out more reliable information. Along with a heart that loves to ask questions, they may have a knack for getting things out of people, scouring social media or just piecing information together.

Approachable – The key purpose of a wingman is to improve their friend's chance of attracting someone, but they can't be undesirable themselves. Having big circles and connections everywhere, wingmen can draw upon them when needed. Their charisma and friendliness will also make it easier for others to trust them for advice.

What's the Sitch?

Now, let's say you've decided that you fit all the above traits, and you'd like to do your first task. Your friend has just contacted you about this stranger at the library, who they think is kind of cute, and wants your help.

As a wingman, you'll find yourself wearing lots of different hats. Although I'm listing them here now, when you actually get to it everything will be all blended together. Just as in other aspects of life, our roles aren't always clear-cut, and we find ourselves doing them without even knowing.

- ❖ **Intel** – Before your friend even begins to pursue someone, your investigative skills will give you some rough ideas of the potential love interest you're dealing with.

- ❖ **Guru** – Your friend will ask you lots of questions about dating, which we covered earlier on in this book.

- ❖ **Back up** – You'll be physically at the same place as your friend while they do their thing. You'll be either providing moral support with your presence, or you'll need to watch the situation and act accordingly.

- ❖ **Support** – You'll not only be providing emotional support for your friend when they're dealing with a break-up or fight, but you'll also be hyping them up before they make the leap.

By the way, you don't necessarily have to act alone. Many people enjoy the benefit of their entire circle helping them to get the love life they want. You can team up with other friends to increase the efficiency of your tasks.

Now, let's break the tasks up one by one.

Intel

When an interest in someone first develops, there's going to be a lot of unknowns. While that's probably what makes it so enticing, as a wingman you need to ground your friend with reality first. And to do that, you can help by assessing the person. In this day and age, finding information about someone has never been easier because of something called <u>digital footprints</u>. By harnessing these digital footprints, coupled with testimonies from real-life people, you'll be able to create a data map of the person.

What type of things make up a digital footprint? Well:

- ❖ Statuses and posts on social media.
- ❖ Tagged photos of them on other people's profiles.
- ❖ Screenshots of their text messages to important people.
- ❖ Account information on forums.
- ❖ Subscriptions to various websites.

If you don't believe how easily it is to track someone with their digital footprint, try it on yourself. Using websites dedicated to finding people, such as Pipl.com, will really surprise or even scare you.

So, using this information, you can start to get an impression of your friend's potential love interest without actually meeting them. Just a disclaimer though, it's super easy to fake your life on social media. People that <u>catfish</u> will know that a lot. So, collect online intelligence with discretion, and don't attempt to deduce any major things (such as life events and personality) from it.

The other way of getting information is of course through testimony. If your friend's love interest is within a local dating pool (so not a total stranger they met in Dubai one summer), then chances are you'll know someone else who knows them. Ever heard of the Six Degrees of Separation? It's a theory that dates all the way back to 1929 and suggests that everyone in the whole world can be connected within six connections. Actually, in recent times, that number's been reduced to four. Crazy, right? Well, this just shows us that it's not as difficult as we think to meet someone that can provide reliable information on a new person. The real difficulty comes from your ability to get close to them and get them to give you information, but that'll be based on your own skill.

So, let's see the intelligence process in action. Let's say your friend is quite a progressive person, and they see a cute guy at the coffee shop. By looking at the person's digital footprint (by finding out their name or twitter handle), you see that he is active on quite a few neo-Nazi pages. Well, that obviously means he won't sit well with your progressive friend, so with this first piece of information, you can already deduce that there will be very strong political incompatibility.

Or how about a less extreme example. Your friend is a bookworm and loves reading most of the major fantasy franchises out there. And they would like to meet someone that is equally enthusiastic about books. They spot a cute guy at the library. Then you find out the guy is strongly interested in footy, video games and that's about it. Even through a clean sweep, you can't find any activity anywhere that shows that he's even remotely interested in reading. Well, one last thing to do is to look at his connections. On Facebook, you can see most of his mates are either gaming buddies or footy teammates. But you know one of them quite well, because you also play video games with them. So you decide to catch up with your friend, and enquire him about mysterious library guy. And that's when you find out that mysterious library guy has started to take an interest in fantasy novels, and therefore started to visit libraries often. Bingo! Using this information, you can then give it to your friend, and hopefully, if they're brave enough, they can strike a conversation with the guy and his newfound interest in books.

Guru

Armed with some basic but helpful knowledge, you can be very helpful to your clueless, love-stricken friend. As a guru – though I like the word 'coach' more – you can guide your friend through the process of hopefully finding love. This can start all the way at the beginning where they need to work on themselves and get into the right mindset for dating. Or maybe they've done all that and just want to know how they can resolve fights better, something like that. Advice will always be helpful no matter what stage they're in.

To give people good advice, you also need to be a good listener (as described in the previous chapter). That way, when you give solutions, you're actually creating a response to the problem instead of just making up a solution for the sake of it.

How do you give good advice? Well here are four things you need to think about, adapted from the Entrepreneur.

1. **Give advice only when asked** – This is one of the core values that make up a wingman. For some people that are especially

enthusiastic about helping someone with knowledge they're good at, they may find themselves spontaneously giving advice, even when the person they're talking to didn't ask for it. That's a huge no-no. Unsolicited advice can easily backfire, because it can be commonly perceived as intrusive and critical. Always let them figure out things themselves first. Maybe guide them along the thought process, but ultimately, if they haven't explicitly asked for your help, stay on the sidelines.

2. **Discuss different options** – When giving advice, ensure that you can give your friend many different choices. Or, at least make them feel like they have a few. This can give you a fallback because, even though you may feel like you're an expert in a certain field of knowledge (in this case, dating), you need to acknowledge that you don't always know best. When offering advice, it's always good to prioritise the information of the person at hand, instead of your own expertise. Remember that, it's an important point.

3. **Think along with them** – Not every problem can be solved with a diagnosis from a textbook. Using empathy and perspective, you can immerse yourself in the problem (not too much though, or you'll be too stressed out) and walk through the thought process. This will be much more effective than persuading your friend to agree with the first viewpoint you come up with. At the same time, guide them through the process along with you. Doing this means that

you'll actually train your friend to be prepared for similar situations in the future, so they won't have to consult you every time.

4. **Have confidence in them** – People usually require guidance because they are experiencing a bit of self-doubt. In their mind, all their different perspectives, instincts and whatnot are all having a big debate with each other. When you offer your friend advice, remind them that you're there to help, but that you have faith in their final choices. Sometimes, all a person needs is someone to tell them that they're on the right track.

It can be frustrating when you can visually see someone in desperate need of advice, but they refuse to listen to it. This is where your own character strengths will come into play. Sometimes, you need to let them figuratively crash and burn. What usually happens is that the person will initially refuse and shun your advice, 'crash and burn', and then come back to you, either blaming you or asking you for help. Look, I get it can be super infuriating. The most human thing for us to do would be to tell them to fuck off. But you have to be the bigger person and be there for them. After all, their judgement was clouded, and they were unable to see what you could see at that moment. And trust me, unless your friend is super problematic, they'll sober up in no time and realise that they should've listened to you, even if they don't admit it out loud.

When I was in high school, I met a couple my age. Let's call them Violet and Lily. They've been together for a year, and were in that super lovey-dovey, saccharine phase of love. You can probably imagine it. After a while of getting to know both of them, slowly we were close enough to start confiding about personal things. I remember once, Violet approached me. She was visibly excited. I asked her what was up, and with a wink, revealed a jewellery box that contained a beautiful matching set of crystal (obviously not actual diamonds, we were broke teens) earrings and necklace. I knew it was for Lily and asked her what the occasion was. And you know what Violet told me? "Next year, at the formal, I'm going to propose to Lily!"

Now hold up here. We were 15. Propose? I was pretty taken aback, to be honest. I asked her if she was sure, and she said that she knew they were young, but she knew she was ready to spend the rest of her life with Lily. I have to say, I was pretty impressed by that statement, but we all know that it was definitely too early. So calmly, I asked her if she was sure about the proposal, and if she knew what the average age was for people being proposed to. Remember, you never give advice unsolicited, so instead I guided her train of thought with questions. After a bit of talking, she finally said, "Oh man, it really is too early. Maybe I should wait." I concurred with her and explained that if they were really meant to be together, they could definitely wait at least until they were out of high school before thinking about proposing. Marriage equality wasn't even a thing yet in Australia when this happened.

Violet and Lily broke up around three months after that incident. Ironically and cruelly, the very reason for the split was commitment based. Lily had to move around a bit and it upset Violet so much that they broke up. So, there's that. Did Violet ever come back to me and say she was grateful I told her to rethink proposing? Nope. But it doesn't matter anyways. She learnt a lesson.

Backup

Ah yes, the field work. Sometimes, when your friend needs extra assistance, you might see yourself having to physically participate. Don't worry; it's not as daunting as you think. If you're naturally a charismatic, observant and witty person, your skills will be greatly beneficial. So what type of things will you have to do when you're providing physical support?

1. **Social support** – For especially nervous people, it's hard to venture to a place full of people that you don't know. It's even harder when your purpose is to pick someone out of the crowd to potentially go out with. Therefore, as their friend, you'll be following them into bars, clubs and parties. It's such a good deal. Even if your friend doesn't do anything drastic by the end of the event, they'd still have had fun knowing at least one person there.

2. **Risk assessment** – This is especially vital if your friend is a girl. You are an extra pair of eyes and ears that can survey the situation. Once you see something off, you can discretely let your friend know, and provide a safe escape route. With this aspect of support being so important, it's going to get its own section later on.

3. **Catalyst –** Being on the lookout for potential people to set up with your friend is quite fun. Immerse yourself into the party, and if you're more conversational and social than your friend, you'll be able to get a good scope of the people at the party. Then, you can devise a method to make sure that the stranger you picked out will cross paths with your friend, subtly or not. Using your icebreaking skills, you can even start off a conversation between the two, and then just slip away when you see they're picking up the pace.

This is an aspect of the wingman's task that you might think you're not necessarily accustomed to. After all, events that have high people density, high risk and high levels of socialising can be daunting even to the most comfortable and approachable people. However, I'd just like to say that every 'hat' requires different skills, so not everyone will be able to master all four immediately. That's fine.

Just going to put this out here, but never lose track of your focus as physical support. When you're someone that loves functions and is highly sociable, you can get too carried away having fun at a club that you forget your goal. This will probably leave you with an angry and awkward friend who feels abandoned. Don't be that person, yeah? The general rule of thumb is that if you're out at a gathering as a wingman, temporarily put your own pursuit on pause. Doing that once or twice won't jeopardise your love life, I promise.

Support

Finally, as a wingman, you'll be most likely providing emotional aid. I mean, if you're their friend, you should probably be doing that already, so it's not that hard. The support you provide can go both ways. When they need a confidence boost or are preparing for a date/asking out/proposal, you'll be hyping them up. When they're hurt after a fight or have just gone through a break-up, you'll be there to help their healing process.

To hype your friend up, well, you shouldn't need much of a guide for that. Perhaps with a bit of ACR and enthusiasm, you'll be able to get your friend to the optimal positive mental state they need before a nervous event. Alternatively, you may also want to calm them down. This will call for techniques like square breathing and maybe a mindfulness conversation if they've gone into full blown panic.

Remember when we talked about the mandala in the self-love section earlier on? That's a mindfulness activity. Another mindfulness technique that will help out the most here is <u>Real Time Resilience</u>, from Comprehensive Soldier and Family Fitness – that's right, soldiers use it! What it pretty much means is that as soon as you get panicky thoughts, you immediately shoot them down.

There are three main strategies:

1. Using evidence and data to prove that the scenario won't actually happen.
2. Reframing the thoughts in a more optimistic light.
3. Creating a contingency plan for worst case scenarios.

So, let's say your friend is freaking out over their first date. I'm going to show you the typical panicky thoughts they might have, and how to use each strategy accordingly:

1. **Thought:** "Oh no, I'm going to accidently say something awkward and I'll feel so embarrassed!"

Response (evidence): "That's definitely not going to happen. You speak publicly as part of your [hobby], and all these years I've known you, you're very good with words."

2. **Thought:** "What if I trip in front of my date in these high heels? I'll look so dumb!"

Response (reframing): "Well, if you do trip, your date might think you're clumsy and cute. Pratfall effect!"

3. **Thought:** "Oh man, it's so warm outside, I'm going to sweat so much and my date will think I'm gross!"

Response (planning): "Well, that's possible, but you won't have to worry because I know you always carry around deodorant in your bag."

See? Pretty easy to understand and circumvent the thoughts.

Alright, so what if your friend needs some emotional support after a negative relationship event? Well, the techniques I gave you earlier about counselling yourself after your own break-up can be used. All you have to do is to walk your friend through each step, but don't actually reveal to them the justification behind the steps and the structure of the guide. There's a reason why some therapists don't like treating other therapists. Sometimes it's better for the person getting help to be in the unknown.

I'd like to remind you that it is not your obligation to counsel your friend if things get to that point, even if you're qualified. You need to be able to set your own boundaries with how available you are to listen. For the extra altruistic bunch, it may be hard to wrap your head around that fact but, as a wingman, your own mental state needs to be clear and unaffected, or else your help will be ineffective. This point will remain true to any interaction you'll have with other people, be it your partner, family or friends.

When to Intervene

The wingman has one more hidden hat. We call it 'hidden' because of the fact that you'll be most likely relaying information to no one during its operation. This is unlike the four other roles we've just discussed, which may see you and your pal pulling strings to get the love interest, or liaising back and forth between your friend and their love interest (who is likely to be your friend as well).

This hidden role is <u>intervention</u>, or as some people on the Internet like to call it, <u>cock-blocking</u>. Sounds like a complete 180 from the very purpose of a wingman right? Well, assuming many people wingman people who they're close to, it would be quite common for wingmen to care about the wellbeing of their friends. Also, learning how to split up a couple or make someone stop pursuing someone will allow your wingman skills to come full circle, and that gives you the complete ability to manipulate the whole situation. But don't worry; it's not as sinister as you think. If you need to intervene it should be for one reason only. And this reason is:

Your friend's wellbeing is being threatened.

Yep, that's it. No ifs or buts. What are not valid reasons for intervention?

1. **You just don't like the person your friend wants to date.**
2. **You don't want your friend to get a relationship.**
3. **Someone else told you to intervene.**
4. **You find the couple annoying.**

To act upon any of the above reasons won't just make you a terrible wingman, but a terrible friend. Some of those points will make you come off as overbearing, immature and jealous.

Of course, there's also a bit of a grey area. If you've had past conflicts with their love interest, have had undesirable relationship history, or straight up have a crush on them as well, then it's not going to be quite clear. At this point, you'll need to sort it out with your friend. Be upfront and honest. Remind them that you are not trying to jeopardise their love life, but also not going to sacrifice your own wellbeing (remember assertiveness). Whatever happens next, will happen.

With such a small dating pool in high school, I've seen the above situation happen all the time. I knew an acquaintance that I'll call Jessica, who liked some guy I'll call Frank. Now Jessica's best friends with Amy. Jessica and Frank hit it off pretty well, but Amy seemed a little unenthusiastic about the whole thing. I asked her what was up, and it was revealed that Amy liked Frank as well! I advised her to talk to Jessica about her own feelings so they could sort it out, and what I got back from Amy was that Jessica understood her feelings and backed off from Frank. I was pretty relieved to hear that, up until Jessica came up to me and asked me and my other friends about pursuing Frank. I put all the facts on the table and said, "Look, if you do go forward with it, it will impact the friendship circles you're in. If you're still on the fence about Frank, I suggest you drop it."

The next day, I found out that she got together with Frank anyway. As you can imagine, Amy was pretty devastated by it. And as I foretold, the group literally scattered like bowling pins. This is one of those moments I've mentioned previously where, as a wingman, you need to be mentally prepared for people to not listen to you. Oh well, at least Frank and Jessica were happy. I've lost contact with them, so I'm not sure how their relationship panned out.

Alright, so back to the main topic. When I'm talking about your friend's wellbeing, I'm talking all aspects: physical, emotional, and mental. This will apply regardless of your friend's progress in love. Let me put it another way for you. Here are some typical scenarios that will call for intervention:

1. You watched your friend's date spike their drink.

2. Your friend is being taken advantage of while in a vulnerable state.

3. You discover a new dangerous fact about your friend's love interest.

4. Your friend is being abused.

5. The relationship dynamic is unethical and potentially dangerous (teens dating 30-year-olds).

Three Types of Risk Perception

For the first three points, the skill you need to help your friend out is called risk perception. Essentially, it refers to your ability to foresee threats and act accordingly. Luckily, it's a skill that can be developed and you'll see yourself preventing dangers from happening before anyone can even see them.

If you're accompanying your friend to a club as a wingman, here's what you should do to maintain good risk perception.

1. **Watch your drinks** – Keep a good eye on both of your drinks. Never leave them unattended Make it a rule between you and your buddies that as soon as you get a drink, keep your glass covered with your hand until you've finished it, and you won't take breaks between a drink that require you leaving it (unless of course your friend can supervise it for you). . There are many opportunistic people in large social gatherings who will watch their targets take their eyes off the drink, and then spike them. Alternatively, in a restaurant or bar setting where your friend is seated one-on-one with their date, drink spiking can still happen. This is called <u>date rape</u>. If your friend is lucky enough to have you supervising a date like that (maybe sitting a few tables away or getting a live feed), then you have the responsibility to watch their drink. In these types of situation, people will most likely wait until the target needs to go to the bathroom or something before striking. By keeping an eye on your friend's date, you can

monitor their drink and text them discretely if they are in danger. But at the same time, it's still good to develop the habit of not drinking things offered by other people and throwing away drinks you've abandoned.

2. **Watch your friend** – When in a situation where your friend will be potentially vulnerable because of a substance, you need to keep your risk perception high. This can be done by reducing your own substance use. I understand, it sucks to not participate when you're invited, so what I'm saying is feel free to immerse yourself into the social gathering, but make sure your substance use while being a wingman is much less than if you were actually at a party just for fun. That means cutting your usual five standard drinks to three or something like that. When watching your friend, there's no need for you to be following them around like a bodyguard. That will affect their interactions with potential love interests, and probably annoy them as well. Keep at a distance but keep them in full view. Create a safety system with your friend that is non-verbal and discrete, such tapping three times on their elbow. This can be used when you can sense unease in your friend. Once you tap them, you two can then improvise a reason for why they have to leave. If your friend's love interest is the host of the party (and things are going bad), make sure your reason to leave wouldn't be solved by sleeping over (and therefore staying in a bad situation).

3. **Watch their date** - While you keep a close eye on your friend, it's also good to watch what their love interest is doing once a while, especially at a party, where everyone can be anywhere at any given time. It'll surprise you how easy it is for people to spike drinks even in places where there is a high people density. Just like reading for uneasy body language in your friend, you can also read any predatory and creepy behaviours of their date. Using the safety system that I mentioned above, even if your friend doesn't feel uneasy yet (again, substance can affect risk perception), you can still let them know that the person is a little suspicious. If they don't necessarily know you that well, it's probably better for you to not introduce yourself earlier on in the night, or your presence will be associated with surveillance. If you do know the person, greet them early on in the party, but don't be close to them the entire time.

Body Language Signs

The way we subconsciously convey information non-verbally is truly incredible. Body language makes up 93% of communication, that means only 7% comes from words. Except for those that have developmental disorders, most of us are all built with an innate ability to read body language. From the very start of life, we already learn what it means to see someone smile and frown. However, as we grow up and experience more complex emotions, it gets more complicated than that. Most of us can still read basic emotions: joy, anger, sadness, excitement. However, to read more into a person's thoughts (which frequently incorporate more than just the basic emotions), extra observance is needed.

In this context, we're going to be looking at three different types of emotional states. They are comfort, unease and danger. Learning these three will be all you really need for risk perception. Since there will be many situations at a party or event where you and your friend can't communicate verbally, predicting their mindset is a good safety precaution. At the same time, suspicious people will never directly communicate their ulterior motives, but can easily give them away through body language alone. By decoding them, you can create a safer environment for your friend and yourself before it's too late.

Comfort
This is a desirable emotion to see in your friend and their love interest. Comfort means that they feel relaxed, happy and, most importantly, safe. This is an emotion that people barely communicate verbally. It would be pretty weird if you sat down in front of a date, and announced, "gee, I feel comfortable".

Proximity – People that are comfortable with each other will decrease proximity. This will mean leaning in during a conversation, moving closer on the chair or turning their face towards the person. Personal space is an almost primal concept that we have as humans. We are programmed to maintain it for safety, and only let in those we trust.

Face – People that are enjoying themselves will have the corner of their mouths slightly upturned. It's not as noticeable as a full smile (which would be kind of creepy), but if you are observant of body language, you'll see it.

Head - The positioning of the head can indicate a person's emotions during conversation. A tilted head indicates curiosity, a head rested on hands means listening intently. Leaning forward, resting your elbows on the table then your head on your hands means focussed listening. All of these indicate deep engagement from the person, which happens when they're comfortable.

Physical touch - Just like the concept of personal space explained in part 6, a person's willingness to break their touch barrier with you is a big indicator of comfort. It could just be things like tapping someone's shoulder, hugging them or touching their arm. The intensity of touch can vary as there are people that don't like touching people regardless of closeness.

Unease

The very opposite of comfort, a mild feeling of threat. A person that feels uneasy during a conversation will show a slight increase in stress. Unfortunately, sometimes society's overbearing focus on politeness (especially for females) can force people to obscure signs of unease when communicating with others. Because of this, it may take a little more observation to detect this emotion in a female friend.

Proximity - Now, instead of closing in distance, an uncomfortable person will increase their distance by either physically leaning back or by putting things between them and the other person. Crossed arms are a big giveaway to a person that isn't 'open', or comfortable with the interaction.

Hands – Your hands, being such versatile limbs, can give away a wide range of things. When a person feels uneasy in a situation, they may subconsciously rub their neck or touch their face. The reason they do this is because of the amount of nerve endings in that area which when stimulated, can lower heart rate and provide comfort.

Feet – Many people already know this, but the positioning of people's feet can indicate many things. When observing a group of people talking for example, you can actually watch and realise that everyone's feet subconsciously point to the most popular person – the leader, you can say – of the group. A person will point their feet away from a person when they feel the need to exit a conversation.

Eye contact – A person's ability to maintain eye contact depends on their confidence. During an uneasy exchange, a person's confidence can be altered as they may feel a loss of control or threat to themselves. Therefore, they may fail to maintain good eye contact with the person they're speaking with. Additionally, they may frequently glance in the same places repeatedly. Watch where your friend looks to. If they glance to you, a person they're comfortable with, or the exit, then you know your friend needs some help.

Danger
People that have ulterior motives don't reveal them straight away. Whether at a one-on-one date or at a large house party, predatory people will always initially mask themselves with friendliness. This

enables them to build trust with a victim. If they are extra experienced, they can become adept at hiding their body language, so be careful.

Face - A predatory person that is thinking about attacking will show signs of adrenaline in their bloodstream. This can show in various ways on the face. As adrenaline is a stimulating hormone that triggers the fight-or-flight response, a person high on it will experience pupil dilation, increased sweat production (not a reliable sign if the environment is humid or warm) and mouth breathing.

Hands - As the exposure of the torso is a sign of weakness and friendliness, a person crossing their arms signals subtle animosity. Alternatively, hands that are constantly in pockets represent our primal habit of obscuring ourselves when being secretive or dishonest. Clenched fists show inner tension and hostility.

Feet - As a way to prepare for sudden action like an attack, humans subconsciously position our feet in a stance called blading. I'm sure you've seen it before in videos of two people engaging in a fight. The person will put their dominant leg behind the non-dominant leg, angling their dominant foot out rather than straight on. It is highly unnatural for anyone to do this combat stance during a conversation, unless of course they plan to take physical action against their target.

Context is a very important factor to consider when reading body language. Just as someone may hate being touched regardless of the person, or how someone may cross their arms because the room is cold, not all body language signs discussed here can be a sure-fire way to know a person's emotional status. That is why we learn all the possible signs to one emotion, in different areas.

While humans have a knack for reading body language, it can't be 100% effective when predicting people's thoughts. After all, there are many factors involved, such as context, a person's ability to hide their body language and your own skills of observation. So, I guess the key takeaway is to judge with your instinct, because that will usually override all of those factors. Maybe the person you and your friend are talking to just doesn't *feel* right. In that case, it's still completely reasonable for you to get out of there. Remember, as a wingman, your friend's wellbeing is a top concern, so it's better to be safe than sorry. Prevention over treatment.

Your Final Dose of Wisdom

You're now almost done with this book. It surely has been a ride, and I hope you've learnt a lot. Below are 100 pieces of wisdom I've discussed in this book, plus a bonus activity. If you couldn't get much out of this book, I hope you can at least take away all the things I say below.

Wingman 101

1. Love is an emotion characterised by a combination of 'feel-good' hormones.

2. The most certain thing in the world is the uncertainty of love.

3. If you're a pre-teen, don't be in a hurry to fall in love.

4. The best way for a teenager to experience romance is to freely explore their identity.

5. Don't put yourself down for not being attracted to someone. We all have different requirements.

6. Fetishisation and shaming is problematic.

7. Labels are like shoe sizes. They can change throughout your life but each previous one got you to where you are now.

8. If you can't imagine a future with someone, then choose 'forget' in the forget/pursuit dichotomy.

9. Your appearance matters, no matter what you think.

10. When you pursue love, focus on the present.

11. Charisma is the most powerful trait a person can have to attract someone.

12. Never date for the sake of dating.

13. There's no need to rush in the road of pursuit. Move when you're ready.

14. LGBT people deserve love, so have hope.

15. There's no single formula for flirting. Like a chess game, it relies on individual input.

16. Keep flirting light-hearted.

17. Pickup lines will never work as intended, but they can be good fun sometimes.

18. Icebreakers are much better than pickup lines and work as a flirting strategy.

19. Like the 20-question method, do life one step at a time with plenty of fallback.

20. Keep all three of your social circles healthy.

21. Your peer's responses don't necessarily indicate your relationship's quality.

22. You may lose bad friends when you date. To weed a garden, you need to rip from the roots.

23. Psychology is like fire. It's very useful but misuse is highly damaging.

24. Choose a first date that has an appropriate amount of socialising with you and just you.

25. Don't involve friends in an activity unless they're reliable.

26. It's important to agree on pacing between you and your partner.

27. There's no need to enforce gender roles when it comes to polite actions. Just do them.

28. Forcing your partner to do things they don't want to, constitutes as sexual assault.

29. High school is a fish tank, university is an aquarium and life after university is the whole ocean.

30. It's best to not date someone from the same school.

31. A person never owes you any feelings, no matter how nice you were to them.

32. The friend zone does not exist.

33. Love is a nice cocktail but don't get too drunk.

34. Understand your partner's love language to maximise relationship quality.

35. Get yourself and your partner to take advantage of the power of touch.

36. Avoid dating for a while if you suffer from love addiction.

37. A relationship should enhance your life, not complete it.

38. Enforcing traditional relationship dynamics helps nobody.

39. The honeymoon phase happens in the first 2-3 years and does not last.

40. Every stage of a relationship can have its own beautiful portrayal of love.

41. Always discuss with your partner about your relationship's online presence.

42. The only reason you two won't meet each other's parents is if it's unsafe.

43. Communication is absolutely vital in a relationship.

44. Sort out early on how you want to celebrate Valentine's Day and your first anniversary with your partner.

45. Check in on your partner in the first six months, and then after the first year check in every anniversary.

46. Relationships never just fall apart spontaneously, but after problems have brewed for too long.

47. Check in on pacing, issues, the future, emotions, things to start and things to stop.

48. Don't panic if you find yourself suffering from love blindness. It's not too late.

49. Red flags of your partner may cause you to blame yourself. Don't fall for it.

50. Most relationships will end in the long haul.

51. A long-term relationship is a form of delayed gratification.

52. The transition between honeymoon and long haul isn't a loss of love, but rather a transformation of it.

53. Your high school relationship will probably fail unless you both ground yourself with reality.

54. Cuffing someone at school is like choosing an apple from one tree in a whole orchard.

55. Make a pledge with your partner about honesty if you lose attraction while at university.

56. Don't use this book to solve your relationship problems. Use your head.

57. It should be you and your partner vs the problem, not you vs your partner.

58. Romance isn't eternal. In fact, nothing is. That's why you need to change along with it.

59. Replace aggravating phrases, and slip in diffusers to help ease the situation.

60. Only say sorry if you mean it.

61. Don't say sorry just because you're supposed to.

62. There are only two fates for a relationship: you die before it ends, or it ends before you die.

63. When you aren't physically attracted to someone, there's no romance anymore.

64. Be mentally prepared before you break-up with your partner.

65. Breaking up is like getting branded. It hurts a lot and leaves a mark that fades with time.

66. Frequency doesn't always correlate with effectiveness when it comes to break-up strategies.

67. There's no need to measure the severity of abuse. Abuse is abuse.

68. It is never your responsibility to stay with an abuser and 'fix' them.

69. A break-up is a loss of a relationship and its future. You need time to mourn.

70. A break-up requires two people, therefore it's never 100% anyone's fault.

71. Don't convince yourself that you're a helpless victim.

72. Love yourself and tell yourself you deserve better.

73. Losing love can actually boost your character growth in something called post traumatic growth.

74. You are your own strongest supporter.

75. There's no need to be shallow when people care about physical attraction.

76. Brush up on dress codes to prevent embarrassment.

77. The way you use colour in clothes matter a lot.

78. Learn to set the table in three ways: basic, casual and formal.

79. Position your cutlery according to your progress in a meal.

80. Every flower conveys a different meaning. Learn that before you send bouquets.

81. Sewing a button is a genderless skill.

82. It's good to know how to waltz.

83. Pretty much everyone appreciates a good photo

84. As soon as you can balance your own needs with others' needs, you've cracked the code.

85. Speak assertively by directly identifying the situation and your responsive feeling to it.

86. Just because you're empathetic doesn't mean you're good at consoling.

87. Your partner's love language can reveal what consoles them the most effectively.

88. No is a complete sentence.

89. Your partner isn't a mind reader and will never be 100% sure what you're feeling.

90. By being kind to everyone else with 'yes', you're being unkind to yourself.

91. Hearing requires just your ears, but listening requires your heart.

92. How you respond to your partner's good news matters.

93. Always ask before you kiss your partner for the first time.

94. The act of kissing relies on all five senses.

95. Being a third wheel isn't a bad thing. In fact, it can help with your own endeavours.

96. The only person that's making you feel resentful about being a third wheel is yourself.

97. Being a good wingman takes more than just knowledge in romance.

98. Prioritise the information at hand over your own expertise.

99. Set your own boundaries when counselling a friend to avoid burnout.

100. You should only ever intervene in a relationship's progress if your friend's wellbeing is being threatened

101. Prevention always beats treatment in risk perception

101 – Make your own Wingman Kit

The bonus information I want to give you is the Wingman Kit. Essentially, it's a bunch of items you should always keep on you when spending time with your partner. Through this book, you've built a mental toolbox, but a physical one is also nice. Your kit should be fully customisable and appropriate to the context. For example, if condoms don't apply to either of you, don't pack any. You'll see what I mean. Some things you can put in your kit include:

1. **Earphones** – Good to share music with your partner. It also looks kind of cute.

2. **Lipstick** (if applicable) – Good for a quick fix after eating or a messy make-out session.

3. **Chapstick** – Maintains you and your partner's lips for peak condition.

4. **Umbrella** – The compact ones work best. A good excuse to stand closer to your partner.

5. **Mints** – Can help you and your partner maintain fresh breath, and hide substance use if needed.

6. **Condoms** (if applicable) – It's better to keep them on you than leave them in your car.

7. **Perfume/cologne** – Good to retouch after a long sweaty day, or get rid of bad scents quickly.

8. **Handkerchief/tissues** – Multipurpose, like wiping your date's tears or dabbing food off their face.

9. **Pocket mirror** - Good to check for things in your teeth, smudged makeup etc.

10. **Stain remover** - Instant stain remover pens are literal life savers for you or your date's outfit.

This list only includes some suggestions of things I come up with. As you wingman yourself, you'll find things that you want to include, and you'll probably come up with your own custom wingman kit that suits you better. That's the great thing about everything in this book, really. Ultimately, it's all about you. Now isn't that exciting?

Closing Words

So, you've read to this very last page now. Congrats. Coming to the end of this book means you're at the beginning of your journey. I hope you've enjoyed reading what I've had to say. To be very honest with you, even if you followed everything here 100% perfectly, I still can't guarantee that you'll have a flawless love life. That's because life has infinite possibilities, and anything can make an impact on how your life runs, just like this book. You're a ship sailing in the vast open ocean, and you'll come across many little things in your voyage that alter the direction of your journey. They may enable you, or they may hinder you. You're young, so you still have many of these experiences yet to experience. This book, your friends, your family; we're all just stars pointing north in the night sky. We are tools providing guidance for your journey in life, but ultimately it is you who controls where to go and what to do.

This book took me approximately six months to write. I only decided to start this project halfway through year 12 because I could see that my high school life was coming to an end. *The Wingman's Handbook* was one of those concepts I'd think about for fun. But with my time in high school running out, I decided to actually make it a reality. Because this book is a collection of my experiences and research, it would actually be more accurate to say that I've been working on this project since 2012, which is a pretty long time for a book to come together, isn't it?

When I first began typing it up, I felt a little doubtful. I'm not a natural writer, and every other writing projects I've had in the past never got completed. But another part of me thought that this time it might be different, because it was a non-fiction book on a subject that I knew a lot about, instead of a novel of a world that I still had to get used to myself. There were definitely some rough patches I had to deal with when writing this book. Because senior schooling making us all bust our ass, there were times when my writing flow completely stopped for months. That's just how it is. But luckily, I survived. Using the remainder of my long summer holiday before I prepare for university, I made my final finishing touches and breathed a breath of life into this book.

So where to now? Well, your life is yours. You're still young, so make the most of it. There's no right or wrong, ifs or buts with your sexual identity. Don't listen to the crushing and restrictive rules of society. They don't know you as well as you do. Explore what love truly means to you. Go experience some romance and some heartbreak. Take all the time you need. Before you go, my dear reader, I'd just like to conclude with an extract from a nice poem by William Ernest Henley:

> *"It matters not how straight the gate,*
>
> *How charged with punishments the scroll,*
>
> *I am the master of fate:*
>
> *I am the captain of my soul."*

www.ingramcontent.com/pod-product-compliance
Lightning Source LLC
Chambersburg PA
CBHW071856290426
44110CB00013B/1164